I AM MORBID

DAVID VINCENT

with Joel McIver

I AM MORBID

Ten Lessons Learned From Extreme Metal, Outlaw Country, And The Power Of Self-Determination

David Vincent
with Joel McIver

A Jawbone book
First edition 2020
Published in the UK and the USA by
Jawbone Press
Office G1
141–157 Acre Lane
London SW2 5UA
England
www.jawbonepress.com

ISBN 978-1-911036-55-5

Jacket design Paul Palmer-Edwards, www.paulpalmer-edwards.com

Printed by Everbest Printing Investment Ltd.
1 2 3 4 5 24 23 22 21 20

TABLE OF CONTENTS

FOREWORD BY
DR. MATT TAYLOR 5

INTRODUCTION 9

chapter one

BE STRONG,
YOUNG MAN 11

chapter two

SUFFER NO FOOLS.............. 38

chapter three

THE MAZE OPENS.............. 65

chapter four

HEAL THE SOUL 90

chapter five

REBIRTH 116

chapter six

HEAVEN AND HELL 141

chapter seven

ONCE MORE MORBID 170

chapter eight

THE ULTIMATUM 211

chapter nine

RELEASE THIS FURY 227

chapter ten

GATHERED FOR A
SACRED RITE 252

DISCOGRAPHY 268

INDEX 269

FOREWORD

So there I was, sitting in a rental car, halfway from Houston to Austin, having just used my Cockney accent to get out of a speeding ticket. It was March 2015, and less than two months had passed since I'd had one of the most bizarre conversations of my life—and that's saying something, considering that I'd just spent the last year or two having daily, hours-long teleconferences covering the large-scale view, as well as the minutiae, of a space-science mission to a comet some five hundred million kilometers from Earth.

This particular chat was different, though—I'll never forget it. I was on one of my regular trips to the European Space Astronomy Centre, the European Space Agency site where all the science-instrument operations are collated, but this was nothing to do with space. It was with someone I had read about, listened to, and had a poster of in my bedroom during college and university days—and I really couldn't believe it.

David Vincent and I were chatting about the *Rosetta* mission, about the upcoming session at the 46th Lunar And Planetary Science Conference in Texas, and the possibility of me joining him at an event he was hosting at SXSW in Austin. In fact, he wanted to conduct an onstage chat about the mission and space in general. Oh, and if I wanted, I could hang out at his house, too …

My long-haired, leather-clad younger self went into meltdown and passed out. Luckily, the shorter-haired, more robust, older version of me just about held it together and sorted out the details for the trip. Immediately afterward I emailed my wife and then my buddy Prizeman, a tattooist, using lots of capital letters to describe what had just happened. I was going to hang out with David Vincent!

Let me explain. I grew up in East London in the UK. In the early 1990s I was a short-haired metal fledgling, a typically awkward kid working at weekends to help get me to university, something I was struggling to achieve. Like many kids, I had been searching for *my* sound, and the identity that only music can deliver—and I had found both with metal. I had a guitar; I had Iron Maiden, Guns N' Roses, and Napalm Death, and a bedroom wall beginning to get covered in band posters. I had metal nights at the Ruskin Arms in East Ham, or the Standard in Walthamstow, where Prizeman and I would nurse a bottle of Newcastle Brown Ale each, peeling off the label until the DJ played something that we could do our follically limited headbanging to.

Another buddy of mine, Kaan Yavuzel, had given me a tape of Morbid Angel's first album, *Altars Of Madness*—and as soon as I heard the introduction of 'Immortal Rites,' I knew that this was something else. Their next album release saw me make the old-school pilgrimage into central London to pick it up on vinyl—there was none of the 'click and download' that you kids have now!

No, this was a few hours invested, and then back home with my new Morbid Angel album, *Blessed Are The Sick* (I even remember the catalogue number—MOSH31). I devoured it. Those crazy timings, the mysterious inlay sheet and album artwork, those weird, ethereal instrumentals … I listened to that album a lot, lying in bed and imagining even being able to create such music.

In December 1991, Kaan, Prizeman, and I went to the Marquee Club in London to see Morbid Angel. It was my first proper metal gig, and it was everything I'm dreamed of—huge energy from the band, the pit, stage-diving and crowd-surfing. I still recall the feeling of horror when, having launched myself from the stage for the tenth or twentieth time, I disappeared into a hole in the sea of hands in the mosh pit and hit the deck … hard. However, almost instantaneously I was yanked back off the floor by someone in the crowd. I gave myself a quick check to see if I was okay, and then I got straight back at it. That metal camaraderie was everything.

This was it. This gig cemented that fact that metal was my music.

This was my crew—and this was my Morbid fucking Angel!

YES!

Over the next few months I spent hours painting my leather biker jacket. Its backpiece was inspired by a large Paul Booth tattoo, underlined by the Morbid Angel logo. Once it was done, it was all I wanted to wear, and come the *Covenant* tour in 1993, I was proud to wear it to the gig.

I'd never have guessed that someday a comet would bring David and me together.

In 2013, I was lucky enough to become part of one of the most awesome space missions ever: the *Rosetta* mission. It was a European Space Agency mission to catch a comet called *Churyumov–Gerasimenko*, or 67P, a primordial object made up of the material that went into the formation of the solar system.

The *Rosetta* spacecraft was launched in 2004 and took ten years to approach its target. By mid-2014, public interest in the mission was growing exponentially, and during the *Philae* landing event in November that year, I was contacted by Alexander Milas, the editor of *Metal Hammer* magazine, who wanted to do an interview with me about the science of the mission, as well as my love of metal music.

Things were super-hectic on *Rosetta*, so we couldn't lock down an interview date, but as luck would have it, Prizeman had gotten us tickets for the Morbid Angel gig in London that December. As he told me, 'Dude—you've got to see Morbid Angel again. David Vincent is the master of the stage!' Alex was also going to the gig, so we arranged to meet up for an interview there.

We arranged to go backstage and meet the band. Of course, I was super-nervous, but David was deeply interested in the mission, and we had a great chat, only cut short at stage time. This interaction between him and me highlighted a crossover of worlds—a synergy between extreme music and extreme science. That night kick-started a fantastic collaboration with Alex, focusing on the overlap between music and space exploration—a project we called *Space Rocks*.

In fact, David enabled a kind of proto–*Space Rocks* interaction when he and I chatted onstage about the solar system and science at an event in Austin during SXSW. It was an unforgettable experience, and testament to his drive and vision that we pulled it off. NASA have subsequently run panels at SXSW, including the Parker Probe mission with my good friend Dr. Nicky Fox, but David and I got there first. Hey, David, maybe we should try and do it again?

It is fitting that I'm finishing this foreword in the very hotel in which I had that teleconference with David some four or so years ago, reflecting on how our very different paths converged. But they did—and here we are, with me writing an unconventional foreword to a suitably unconventional autobiography.

So settle back, ready yourself, and remember …

Stay extreme. Stay Morbid!

\m/

Dr. Matt Taylor, MPhys PhD DIC
Rosetta Mission Project Scientist
European Space Agency

INTRODUCTION

Welcome to my autobiography. We're going to have some fun over the next couple of hundred pages—and maybe we'll gain a bit of wisdom together.

I didn't want to write a conventional autobiography. You know the kind of book I mean, where a rock musician gets famous, falls from grace (ha!), and then recovers after some kind of redemption. I've been through some of that stuff, but I like to think there's more to my years on the planet than the old familiar tale. Many of those stories seem to be about drugs, addiction, rehab, and relapse, but that was never my issue. My challenges weren't any less challenging than anyone else's; they just manifested themselves in different ways. This book is about what I've learned, which is a lot, but never enough.

As I see it, the society we live in right now needs to evolve, and fast. On the one hand, I feel really lucky and inspired that I've grown up around one of the biggest technological revolutions that we've ever known, and that things are moving at warp speed now. I always remember the old *Star Trek* TV series, and I realize how just about everything on that show has come into reality: communicators, medical scanners, maybe even teleportation one day. All of these things seem plausible, and because of the advances in science and medicine that I've seen, and because of how rapidly some of these things have happened in my lifetime, it gives me hope that all of these things are doable.

We used to think that science fiction in the old days of black-and-white cinema was unbelievable, but so much of it has been attained. Technological revolutions all start with a dream or fantasy, and then some crazy individual comes along and makes them happen. Look at the speed with which genetic manipulation has come along over the last few years, for example; they've found certain disease-causing genes, and we're on the cusp of being able to treat those familial traits *in utero*.

We've advanced so far in a certain number of areas that one could reasonably deduce that any of these things are right around the corner, because the evidence is there to suggest that they will be, knowing that computer power is accelerating as fast as it is. So I have hope, and the evidenced belief, that we're going to continue along this path.

At the same time, as a species we don't exactly behave well. We treat the planet almost as badly as we treat each other, and most of us don't take the time to think about what lies ahead. A lot of people aren't active participants in life: they're passive participants, and they only seek ways to distract themselves from life and keep the dollars flowing.

In this book I want to address those things, looking back at my own personal evolution from the kid I used to be to the man I am today. You may or may not agree with what follows, but, either way, you're going to enjoy hearing about the crazy stuff that happened to me. I can barely believe it myself.

Thanks for coming along for the ride.

David Vincent
Austin, Texas, 2019

chapter one

BE STRONG, YOUNG MAN

"When you're a kid, you don't know what lies ahead, so there's no better time to focus, keep your eyes and brain open, and make sense of the world as best you can."

I officially parted ways with the womb at high noon on April 22, 1965, in Pompton Plains, New Jersey, into an empty nest of love and anticipation. My folks had been married for four years and had been trying for a child for several years already. They chose to go on a vacation to Canada, where purportedly I was conceived. Maybe it was the good vacation sex, or maybe it was something in the water? In any event … blame Canada!

Dad was a first-generation immigrant whose parents arrived in the USA from Austria just after World War I. Mom's paternal side had been here for quite some time, while her maternal side were also rather recent immigrants from Italy.

When my parents got together, my father was fresh out of the Air Force. He was a fighter pilot and had been involved in a plane crash, although he wasn't the pilot on that occasion. When he and my mother met for the first time, he was in a full leg cast.

My mom was a registered nurse, but she took a break from her career to raise me and later my two younger brothers. My father took a job as a sales associate for a large chemical company and got promoted quite a bit, and when each promotion came along, it always involved a move. We moved several times in the early days. I started kindergarten and first grade when we lived in a suburb of Chicago, and eventually we arrived in Charlotte, North Carolina, when I was in fourth grade.

When we got to Charlotte, my parents didn't want to go anywhere else. My dad once mentioned to me that there had been an opportunity for a promotion that would have involved moving to South America, but they didn't want to go. The sociopolitical climate down there wouldn't suit them while they were raising kids.

Growing up, I wouldn't say that I ever really fit in, although I always had friends; my interests were not the same as those of certain people of my own age category. I was always into my own thing, and I was encouraged to be that way by my parents. I was taught always to question facts and not to accept the world at face value. I wasn't grateful to them for such advice at the time, because you never really appreciate good teaching until its effects make themselves apparent in your adult life.

When I was young I would go dove-hunting with my father, so I grew up surrounded by a culture of self-reliance and acquiring skills when it came to using tools. I had my first shotgun when I was eleven, and it really worked well in an open area like a cornfield. The birds tended to dart suddenly from cover, so we needed to wear camouflage and react fast. My dad had this really old gun with a long barrel and a full choke, and he's a good shot. You heard all these people shooting automatic shots, and the bird just dodged them, but then my dad would stand up and shoot once—*Boom!*—and the bird would drop.

Dad taught me proper gun safety and technique, and it was good father-son time. I was taught, and I still believe, that if you take an animal's life it should be for food: otherwise, you're disrespecting the animal. The same goes for fishing, although oftentimes that's just a catch-and-release sport. You get the fish, say hi to it, and put it back in the water. No harm, no foul.

There are people who don't like hunting, but I don't care; they can not like it as much as they want to. A lot of people are against certain things, but they don't mind going to McDonald's and eating something that looks like a hockey puck but is apparently meat.

To me, it's give and take; you feed the land and the land feeds you. I personally wouldn't go and hunt a big animal such as a lion, of course; sport hunting is not for me. But everyone is different. In Korea, for example, people eat dogs, and I wouldn't do that, but it is not up to me to say that something is wrong for everyone simply because I wouldn't do it.

I vehemently dislike McDonald's and the rest of the fast-food chains. The food is awful, and it's not healthy. I'll eat a burger if I have to, but I don't like the notion of fast food and how it's become so prevalent. Even if I'm hungry, I'll see the golden arches and not even register the idea that they are a food source. On tour, where decent food is often scarce, I'm frequently the only person in our group who won't eat there, but I don't need their support to do what I do. I try to stay disciplined about these things.

I was a Boy Scout as a kid, and I did a lot of outdoor camping. I learned those skills because I wanted to learn them. They're important. If you're stranded in the woods with nothing but a pocketknife and a compass, are you going to be able to eat? What's going to be poisonous and what will save you? You may never have to use these skills, of course. You may also keep a firearm for self-protection, but you hope you never have to use it. I've never heard anyone complain that they were too well prepared.

If society breaks down, how long would the average person cope under adverse circumstances? I don't know that people spend much time thinking about this. I have a lot of friends who have the same attitude as I do, but also a lot of friends who, in the case of an apocalypse, would be fucked. How passively do people think? How many people ever give consideration to a *plan B*, apart from watching a TV program where this is the theme? If Y2K had turned out to be a disaster, how would people have fared? How did people fare who ignored the warnings to evacuate New Orleans when Hurricane Katrina was on its way? Very little thought is given to the skillset that people need to save themselves and their families.

Nature can kill us very easily. Here's a recent example that came about during the writing of this book.

Three nights before I was scheduled to fly to England to record an album with my new band, Vltimas, I was at a friend's house, and they were having a cookout. There were a lot of families there with kids, and at one point my friend came up and told me that he was worried because he thought there was a rattlesnake near the outhouse.

I looked at him and said, 'You *think* we have a rattlesnake, or do we actually have a rattlesnake?'

He said, 'We actually have one.'

I suggested that we find the snake and relocate it, as I didn't want to kill it; they're useful, as they eat rats and other things that you don't want around your house. Snakes are much less loathsome than rats, in my opinion.

Now, I've caught snakes all my life, and I admit that I was experiencing a certain level of intoxication at this point in the evening, so I began confidently searching for the snake using my cellphone light in the dark. I don't recommend doing this, as it didn't work out in my favor.

I found the snake and moved to pick him up just behind the head, but at the last second he inched forward just enough to come back on me and bite me a couple of times on my right hand, grazing my middle finger and then taking a nice juicy chunk out of my thumb.

It didn't hurt at first, but when the poison started to do its work, the pain became incredibly intense. At first I said, 'I'll be all right, I'll go to the doctor in the morning,' but I was told, 'No, you're going now.' So I got a ride to the hospital, and because I was so relaxed I didn't get too excited, although everyone else was waving their hands around and going, 'Oh my God!'

At the hospital, I lay down with my clothes and boots on, and they said to me, 'Sir, you might want to get comfortable, because you're going to be here for a while.' I said, 'Nonsense!' because I wasn't taking it as seriously as I should have been.

It was worth taking seriously, though. I spent five days in the ICU and was administered eighteen vials of anti-venom, which is a lot. It had been a significant bite. It turns out that juvenile snakes don't know how to measure their venom, so when they bite they give it all to you. Adults know how to hold back, and they just give you a little bit—so the bigger the snake, the less problematic it is, apparently.

The swelling in my hand got really bad. People have lost their lives after rattlesnake bites, or had legs amputated, so I consider myself fortunate that I had good, prompt care. I have some residual effects, and I'm still working on therapy for my hand every day. It turned completely black for a good month, and I had some challenges at first, because I had shows to play. Thankfully I'm a finger player on bass guitar, because there was a time when I couldn't hold a guitar pick. I couldn't feel it; it felt as if my big toe was attached to my thumb.

There was a chance that it would get considerably worse, and that the doctors might consider amputation. I guess I'm fortunate that this didn't happen, because with only one hand there's no reason for me to be here. I said, 'If you don't fix this hand, you don't need to worry about anything else,' and they were a bit disturbed by that. It's fine now, although I have some scars.

So, yes—nature can kill you. And it will kill those of us who are not prepared for it.

When I think of my earliest memories, they're always about music. I was really into it. I have memories of always listening to the radio and always wanting to hear more music. I was six years old when Don McLean's 'American Pie' came out, and I memorized it verbatim. I would sing along with it; I loved the way it came up and came down, even though I was too young to understand the story of it and what McLean was trying to get across. To this day, I haven't forgotten that song.

Some people have a photographic memory; I have an audiographic memory. I can't remember names to save my life, unless someone's had a really big impact on me, but commercial jingles will stay with me for life. As a kid I'd hear stuff, and I'd want to stay glued to it. This was before I learned to play music myself. I would listen to songs over and over again.

My grandmother gave me a little record player, along with some records by *Sesame Street* and Disney and so on—just fun songs for kids. I didn't dislike that, but I much preferred Black Sabbath and Jimi Hendrix. A friend who was two years older than me lived behind us, and his brother was four years older than him, and this brother had all this stuff that blew me away. I would borrow records and listen to them *ad nauseam*.

I hear hooks and I remember them—sometimes I'm haunted by them, actually. They're part of the background static I experience where there's always a song playing in my head. I'll walk around the house and sing songs to the pets, and I'll write songs when I'm sitting around the campfire with some friends, especially if there's a guitar around and I've had a few drinks.

My dad and my brothers aren't as musical as I am, although my dad has an accordion that his father gave him, and which he'll bust out every now and then. He also plays a little harmonica, like his father did, but it's not an important thing for him. My dad's sister was musical, though, and her oldest son—my cousin—plays guitar. My musical skills mostly come from my mom. She has a nice voice and is also a pianist and organist. She tells me that when she was pregnant with me, she'd walk around the house and play music, and she thinks that may have conditioned me to enjoy music.

My grade school was a Catholic school, and it was pretty gentrified, with everybody being from a similar socioeconomic background; my parents paid a lot of money to have us go there. I was a good student at first, which is to say that I was interested in the subjects that I was interested in. If there was a good teacher who I identified with and who I respected, rather than someone who was simply going through the motions, I liked the subject.

I had a few history professors that were really good. A lot of history is simply based on memorizing facts and dates, and I cared much less about that stuff than *why* things happened, and what we can take from them. How we can apply what has happened, in the case of events that we don't want to happen again?

Later on, I had a professor in college who didn't care about any memorization of anything. If you had the dates wrong, it didn't matter. He was all about why things happened, what their outcomes were, and how we can relate them to any current situation today. He'd set up these mock situations where you're the President of the United States, and you're faced with a global social or economic challenge. What would you do, how would you negotiate yourself out of it, and what things can you point to historically that give you insights into making the best decision?

That kind of stuff really spoke to me, because it was all about deductive reasoning, which is not often taught these days because it makes you too smart. Teachers don't want you picking out any problems, they want you to just go along and let them take care of everything for you. For that reason, the subjects that were important to me were literature, English language, history—the liberal arts.

I found math boring. I wasn't interested in the intricacies of calculus and trigonometry, and being a rocket scientist is not within my sphere of interest. I was into what I was into, in a natural, organic kind of way. I scored well in the subjects I liked and poorly in things that I didn't care about. For that reason—and because my boredom led me to create mischief—I was kicked out of grade school in 1978, when I was thirteen, and went to a public school.

It was difficult to adjust because now I was around a demographic that I hadn't been around before. My brothers got some heat from me being the black sheep, which made it a little difficult for them. In hindsight, I'm apologetic about that; not for the things I did, but rather that there was blowback on others. At the time, I didn't care, but later I understood that if my negative behavior tarnished someone else's opportunities, that's not good. They're both doing well in life, fortunately.

I felt as though my new school was beneath me, because I was already ahead of my class when I joined in midyear. I remember being issued some books, and I looked at them and said, 'I've already done this.' But I was told that this was where my class was, and that this was what I would be doing. In theory, they could have bumped me up a year, but there was no motivation for them to do so; government schools are a conveyor belt, designed to move people through the system. They have a predetermined way of doing that, and there is no room for objections.

I took a couple of elective courses that were more advanced, but by that point I was bored and not into it. My attitude was not helpful, of course, and so the mischief redoubled. Something disruptive was constantly going on around me. There was a list of the usual suspects on the classroom wall—*The following students must report to …*—and my name was always on the top of the list.

A lot of my pranks involved fireworks, because I was fascinated with them when I was a kid, at New Year's or on Independence Day. They were illegal in North Carolina, but Charlotte is right on the border of South Carolina, where they're legal, so there's a sign that says *Welcome to South Carolina*, and literally ten feet beyond that there's a shop called Colonel Frank's Fireworks, or whatever, stocking anything that you could imagine. We'd roll down there and stock up on all the goodies, and I'd come up with ways to disrupt things at school.

In today's climate, any of these things would be considered terrorist activities, but we were just kids being pranksters back then. We'd bring fireworks to school and find times to set them off. Sometimes one of us would get caught, sometimes not. It was funny because of the reaction when we were sitting in class, and you heard an explosion in the distance.

The assistant principal knew we were responsible; he pretty much had my class schedule memorized. Something would happen, and he'd come by thinking, *I've got you now!* and bust the door open and look over at my desk. If I was there he'd be like, *Dammit!* because he knew I was involved somehow. He just *knew*.

One time, we went all-out and set up a multi-front assault on two different floors in a couple of different halls. We knew which lockers weren't being used, so we packed these things with fireworks—several in each. These were fireworks that didn't just go *Boom!*, they lasted quite a while—strings of firecrackers, rocket packs, whistling effects, that kind of thing. We set them up with a lit cigarette so that as it smoldered its way down it lit a bunch of different fuses.

Once this was all set up, we went to the lunchroom and sat together, so that we were all well in place when the melee started. When it began, you could hear it from miles away. It seemed that the noise would never end; when one firework went off, another one would start.

It just so happened that the assistant principal was in the same area of the lunchroom as we were, so he knew that we were at lunch. All this chaos was going on, with kids running around screaming and laughing. Of course, we were all sitting there with proper table manners, napkins on our laps. He was determined to get to the bottom of this, but none of the other kids would say anything.

This was the one time that my parents were required to go down to the school, because I got suspended for 'conspiracy.' I'd been suspended before, for smoking on school grounds. I did it constantly. They'd confiscate the cigarettes, but I didn't care; I'd just go and get more.

There was no evidence whatsoever that I had done anything wrong this time, but the assistant principal knew I was responsible.

My parents asked me, 'What did you do?'

I answered, 'I was eating lunch.'

They asked, 'Do you know anyone that did something wrong?'

I said, 'Well, you hear stuff around school, but do I say things about people if I don't know that they're true? I don't think so.'

My dad agreed. 'You don't tell stories about people if you don't actually know they're true,' he said, and then he went down there, saying, 'What the hell is this *conspiracy* nonsense?'

It became a cat-and-mouse game in the end, with me trying to find more and more creative ways to break the rules and throw a wrench in the system, simply because I was bored, and also because it was funny to watch the reaction of the system.

In retrospect, I wasn't a particularly bad kid; I never stole anything, although I knew people who did. I was taught not to steal, and never saw a reason to do so.

I wasn't a big drug user, either. I smoked some weed for the first time at the age of twelve or thirteen, but it didn't become habitual. I liked the way that music sounded when I was high, but I was more interested in having fun and testing the system to see how far I could push it.

Could the system have worked for me? No, because it wasn't set up that way. That's like asking if you can go to McDonald's and get a filet mignon with hollandaise sauce. To expect that from them would be idiotic.

My savior was Alice Cooper. Back then, nothing spoke to me as much as the spooky horror aspect of his music, even when I was as young as six or seven years old. For Alice, a love song would be 'I Love The Dead,' which had a creepy feeling that I loved. When his *Welcome To My Nightmare* album came out in 1975, I loved it, and I wore out several copies on my little kiddie record player.

I also really dug B-movies and exploitation films. I'm really into old Hammer horror movies; I loved anything to do with Vincent Price and his Shakespearean acting, and I was fascinated by the overly red blood that Christopher Lee has in all those old Hammer movies.

Later, I discovered KISS. As I was so into Alice Cooper, the first time I saw them in some music magazine in a store, I thought, *Oh my God, it's four Alice Coopers!* When I actually heard the music, I didn't like it at all. I'm now a KISS fan, because I got into them later when I relaxed and got into girls, but when you're six or seven years old you're not thinking about girls.

My music tastes evolved from those two bands. I liked Deep Purple and Grand Funk Railroad, and I heard Led Zeppelin on the radio a lot. I saw Ted Nugent a few times in concert, as well as Aerosmith and Steppenwolf. I liked Blue Öyster Cult a lot, too, and I even liked Yes, even though that's not children's music. I remember getting a compilation called *Heavy Metal*, which had a lot of music on there that wasn't really metal, like Buffalo Springfield. But I always liked a lot of different stuff, including my parents' albums. I wanted to hear any and all music, because hopefully it would be something that I liked.

Obviously, I loved Black Sabbath and Judas Priest, and whatever the heaviest thing was that I could find. Iron Maiden sounded really disjointed to me at first; it took me a moment to hear that it was heavy, but when I started to appreciate the bass playing, that did it for me.

Back in the seventies, radio was much more diverse than it is today. What was considered pop music might be Carl Douglas's 'Kung Fu Fighting' or Black Sabbath's 'Paranoid,' and rock'n'roll radio had a much broader palette than it does today, when everything is so very calculated. The DJs would be actual disc jockeys who would play records. Nowadays they're just personalities with predetermined playlists that are fed to them off the internet. Most radio stations don't even have a CD player—let alone a record player—in the damn studio, so no one's a DJ any more.

Music was a journey that I wanted to take, so I really tried to educate myself about not just the latest thing but also what led to it. I'd ask myself, *Where am I hearing this tone? Who are the pioneers?* There was a lot of pioneering in music and film and general thought in the seventies, and I don't think that decade gets as much credit as it should in that sense. Grindhouse films with grainy textures and generally unhappy endings—such as *The Texas Chainsaw Massacre*, *Vanishing Point*, *Easy Rider*, and *Death Race 2000*—all became very influential, and of course the original *Star Wars* has produced a thriving franchise that is still running strong today. Musically speaking, bands such as KISS, Led Zeppelin, Deep Purple, and the like cemented the foundations of hard rock, whose offspring would ultimately evolve into metal. It was a great time, culturally speaking.

I look back on this part of my life as a really good time. I was ahead of the curve, musically, so I went back and listened to all the Woodstock-era stuff and really tried to get a grasp on the mentality of the times. I didn't understand anything about the war in Vietnam because I was too young. I'd heard about it, and it was in the news a lot, but I knew nothing about it.

In the late seventies, the charts were full of punk rock, which I liked, and disco music, which I didn't. I liked a little bit of funk—The Ohio Players were a band that I enjoyed, with good bass and interesting beats. Blues used to be so good, but we've lost a lot of the greats. B.B. King was a tremendous, soulful, spiritual player. I don't know what happened to high-quality soul music, although I do like R&B singers like Erykah Badu, who has a very passionate, instinctual voice. The *Blues Brothers* movie got me into a lot of this music.

As for hip-hop, it never really spoke to me until NWA came out in the eighties—it was a whole new thing that was fresh and interesting. I'd never heard anything like it; I remember thinking that they were pushing some boundaries with the lyrics, in the same way that extreme metal did back in the day.

In punk rock, I liked The Misfits and the hardcore DC stuff. I loved Black Flag and Minor Threat and Iron Cross. I liked the energy. It wasn't so much about the musicianship per se but about the attitude. It seemed that all of the so-called great musicians didn't have that energy. I was always trying to find something that I didn't know. I've tried to get metal people to understand the energy of punk, but usually they'd say that it just sounded like a bunch of noise.

Soon I started learning to play music myself. I started on upright bass in the school orchestra in third grade, when I was nine years old. I liked it because you could get out of class to do the music lessons, and also because there was a girl that I liked in the orchestra, so I decided to do it, too. They needed a bass player, but I didn't yet take it seriously; that instrument was a beast to get on and off the school bus, and what they were teaching us to play was not the kind of music that I was interested in.

Still, my upright bass studies lasted a while, and they ended up being even more interesting to me because I was always auditioning for parts. Schools had pretty good music programs back in the day, and they'd do recitals where there would be a theme that the music teacher would come up with. We'd all find our spot, and those who cared about music were encouraged to be a part of it.

I was a singer, too, and I always tried out for vocal solo parts. I was probably the best candidate for it, but because of my disciplinary record they would often overlook me and choose someone else—even though I did a better job during auditions, and I knew it.

My mom tells me that I decided to become a performer when I was three years old. 'All you used to say was that you wanted to have a truck, and then you'd put a band in it, and you'd go around and play songs,' she once told me. Other kids wanted to be a fireman or a policeman or whatever. Not me.

I also did a little bit of acting at school, but the instructional side of it needed a different mindset to mine. It was a little too dainty for me. They brought a classical approach, as opposed to, *Here's a character; let's let his personality lead the way.* It was a variety-show approach, with dancing and so on, and I had no interest in it. Later, I came to appreciate it a little more because of what folks like Alice Cooper did, bringing a sort of Broadway approach to their music, but at the time it wasn't on my radar.

My voice went low at a really early age, maybe even when I was seven or eight. My parents used to listen to a group called The Kingston Trio, who played a folksy, calypso style of music, with three singers who would do almost a barbershop trio. They'd sing low and high, similar to a gospel style. I would memorize all the parts, but I always liked the bass parts best. It was comfortable and natural for me, because I heard bass.

When you listened to Black Sabbath, or Alice Cooper's original band, or Grand Funk Railroad, with the way those records were mixed in the seventies, you really heard the bass. It was sometimes the loudest thing on the record. It just sounded really good to me. It was a very organic thing, and ultimately I feel more at home with bass because it's part of the resonance of my being. It makes sense.

I had an uncle and some cousins who had guitars, and I'd sing while they played, and they started showing me some chords. I was interested in this, and I liked it, because rock music spoke to me more at that time than band or orchestra. They didn't have a rock-music program at the school; it was all typical marching-band music and the like. You could select French horn or oboe or trumpet on the request form, but I always filled in my own thing—*electric guitar*. There is a need for all of those classical instruments, but modern music is also a part of that need, and yet I don't think that need was seen in my school back in the seventies.

After a while I bought a bass guitar, because that's what I wanted to play. The one thing I wish I'd never sold is that bass, which was a Gibson EB3. I picked it up second-hand and, although the sound wasn't great, I was firm that I was going in that direction.

Still, I had a lot of hobbies, so I didn't get serious about bass for a while. My high school had a really good auto-mechanics class that lasted three years. In the first year, when you were a sophomore, you had an hour of classroom instruction, and every now and then you'd take a trip down to the garage. In year two, you'd have the hour in class and an hour in the garage, and in year three it was just three hours in the garage.

I wasn't there for year three, and I was only there for part of year two, but the teacher for the class—an old redneck guy who was hard on some students and easier on others—let me get away with murder. Kids would walk into class late, and he'd be really hard on them, but I'd roll in late, and he'd say, 'Why are you late, Vincent?'

I replied, 'I had to walk Rhonda to class.'

He thought this girl Rhonda was cute, so he let me get away with it.

My father was quite strict with me as a child. He hadn't strayed far, culturally, from his Germanic roots in this respect. I learned my grandparents were fairly strict with my father and his siblings as well. They were always really nice to us kids, but it's interesting to know that this strictness seemed to run in the family.

You think back to those times, and it seemed that people from Germany and Austria were culturally strict and authoritarian. That was how it was, although my dad was a little mellower than that, and I'm considerably mellower still, but it was hard for him and me to see eye to eye, because in his opinion things had to be a certain way—and that's just the way they were. There wasn't much room for argument, as he saw it.

These things annoyed the shit out of me when I was a kid, but as an adult, I'm absolutely grateful for some of the things that were taught to me. I've told my parents as much, and it brought my mom to tears, because, as you've read, I had something of a discipline problem at school. Again, I was just bored.

Another challenge for me was that my parents are Christian folks, and, while I'm religious, I'm not a Christian. My father told me a long time ago that, had he known that allowing me to take music lessons would have led to Morbid Angel, he never would have allowed it.

This all came to its logical conclusion in 1982, when I was sixteen. At school, I felt that I was being profiled by the regime. I stood out; I had long hair, unlike anybody else apart from the druggies, who had no ambition. I was disengaged at this point, because I was just thinking about music, so I played the system to minimize my required attendance.

At the beginning of each year, you could set your own schedule of what classes you would do and where you wanted to position them. There was a lottery, and it either accepted your schedule or it didn't. I set my schedule up to where I didn't have a first period each day, so I'd roll into school an hour after everybody else, which was technically not permitted—but somehow they accepted it. After lunch, there was a vocational class, and if you had a job, that would count as a credit. I did have a job, so if I wanted to I could take off after doing only three classes a day.

What threw a wrench into this setup was that they were having some problems in the parking lot. I'd come rolling in when I was scheduled to roll in, and they'd say, 'What are you doing?'

'I'm coming to school,' I replied.

'Well, you're late,' was the answer.

'No I'm not.'

When the staff checked on it, they realized that I wasn't late per the schedule, so they made a point of antagonizing me. They'd come up and say, 'How are you doing today, David?' and I'd be like, 'Do I know you?'

They wanted me to know that they were watching me, even though I was barely in school; I was a ghost. Then they had the school guidance counselor come up and say, 'You're not gonna have enough credits to graduate,' and even though I told them I'd filled out the form like everyone else did, they said, 'We don't know how this slipped by the administration.'

They wanted to get my father involved, and I realized that this whole thing was not working out any more. I was done with it.

My father and I talked.

'I don't feel comfortable at school any more,' I told him. 'I don't have anything in common with any of these people, and I'm ready to move on.'

'You're not quitting school,' he told me. 'If you're under my roof, the rule is that you finish your education.'

In hindsight, he had my best interests at heart, but I don't think he really knew who I was, because we're very different people. I thought about what he'd said, and I said to him, 'You know, you're right. You have every right to say what happens under your roof. For that reason, I'm gone.'

I genuinely agreed with him. I don't remember many conversations verbatim, but I remember that one. Still, my response wasn't the response that they expected, and after I moved out a few days later, relations with them would be difficult for a while. To both of our credit, we grew a lot. I'm thankful that my parents and I now have a wonderful relationship.

"Looking back, I know that it had simply got to the point where my dad had to view me as an adult. There's no such thing as a parenting handbook, because we're all such dynamic creatures with different personalities. As soon as you write the definitive parenting handbook, you're going to have a kid who defies all that logic, and I guess I was that kid."

IMMORTAL RITES

FROM *ALTARS OF MADNESS*, 1989

Gathered for a sacred rite
Subconscious minds allied
Call upon immortals
Call upon the oldest one to intercede
Rid us of our human waste
Cleanse our earthly lives
Make us one with darkness
Enlighten us to your ways

From churning worlds of mindlessness
Come screams unheard before
Haunting voices fill the room
Their source remaining undefined
Shadows cast from faceless beings
Lost for centuries

Lords of death, I summon you
Reside within our brains
Cast your spells upon our lives
So that we may receive
The gift of immortality
Bestowed on those who seek you

I love this song. It's a freeform ritual, very organic, and a nice welcome that sets the tone. It's almost a seance. In fact, 'Seance' was going to be the original title. It's really moody—and it works perfectly. It was our set opener for many years, and the audience identified with it; I clearly recall it going down incredibly well at Morbid Angel's first major show on night one of the infamous Grindcrusher Tour in the UK.

This was our first visit abroad, and although it was a bit of a culture shock for the band, I can honestly say that we were somewhat of a culture shock to the English audience as well. We simply had our way of doing things, which was much different to the ways of the other bands. It could have been cultural, spiritual, or otherwise—suffice to say that we were on our own planet, wherever we traveled. The press at the time featured a lot of commentary about this, and I recall being pleased to hear it. It was our goal, after all, to be ourselves, without being too concerned with how others did things. It was a source of strength and confidence that remains a huge part of my foundation.

SUFFOCATION

FROM *ALTARS OF MADNESS*, 1989

Laugh at the tragedies
Mock with disrespect
Goats under rule of father time
Leeches pass judgment on their fellow kind
And die when their inner self goes astray
Alas, I pay homage to the ancient ones
Speak my name!

Raise the staff of the morbid priest
Descend into the fires of the true law

Suffocating evil smoke arise
Cleansing the masses of iniquity
Cauldrons blaze in sanctifying ritual
Vile crematory burns my eyes

Mortals filled with despair
They quest to foresee their fate
Caverns below await the wine to flow
Rape the harvest of souls
I watch in awe as the crucifiers march
Killing time, killing all I see
Another moon rise, human waste
Screaming, 'Why hath thou forsaken me?'

This song is based on a true story. We were living in a big old house in Charlotte, and there were rats everywhere, because there were all sorts of openings and ways to get in. The band had a pet pit bull, Butcher, who was a really good rat hunter. He'd catch hundreds of them, along with a lot of feral stray cats that were around because there were so many rats. Possums, too, and even some frogs. Butcher would go after anything he saw. We'd say to him, 'Butcher, look at this mess!' but he'd be all proud of himself.

We had a metal trashcan in the backyard, and we threw all the corpses in there. One night we gave them all a proper Viking funeral and set them on fire. The smell was just unbelievably putrid—truly vile. The 'suffocating evil smoke arise' line in this song came directly from this experience. When we vacated the premises, some people that we knew took over the residence, and the trashcan was still out there in the yard. Years later, one of them told me that they were so disgusted with the thing that they put a lid on it, dug a big hole, and buried the whole damn thing, because nobody wanted to mess with it. I got a little chuckle out of that.

Butcher was a great dog. He used to sit and watch us rehearse, and we all loved him. Pit bulls are great dogs, despite their reputation; it's really their owners who are the problem. If you own one, you have to train their natural tendency to fight out of them. People will argue with me about that, but I've been around a lot of pit bulls, and I know what I'm talking about. They're sweet, but they're also knuckleheads, and they're naturally very dominant.

VISIONS FROM THE DARK SIDE

FROM *ALTARS OF MADNESS*, 1989

Dark eyes, shadows grim
They come for me
Midnight chimes, blackened earth
The evils rise
Pits of hate open wide
Chasms of my dreams
Last of chimes, monks arrive
And take my mind again

Waste polluted memories
Acid rivers flow
Vigil for this land's decay
Sounding from below
Dogs of war, Satan's own
Plotting all their sins
Weapons aimed at liberty
My vision, no-one wins

Take my mind
All the way
The dark side calls
I shan't resist

Men forever rot in pain
Mind machines control
Toxic rains scouring brains
Victimizing souls
Winds of war suffocate
Voodoo in the sky
Breathe the gases, breathe no more
My vision, all will die

Cut myself and release the blood
Pains of a thousand years
Pathetic sights, journey's end
Descent into another world
My time has come to meet me

Masters … all the corporate lords
I'm not afraid to face all their
Trials, slavery, in the end they'll
Still have no power over me

Daylight shines blind my eyes
Waken to another day
Tribulation now has passed
But the dreams remain
Walls of sleep fade away
Abandonment of wonders
Monks of knowledge bid farewell
And leave me with these visions
From the dark side

This is a track that I've recently put back into the set because I feel close to it. It's the oracle speaking: it's the most sociopolitical song I've ever written. Even Digby Pearson from Earache, who is a punk-rock guy, made a comment about that, the first time he read the lyrics. He said, 'Man, this is really socially conscious,' and I agreed that it was. I'm talking about the corporate lords and how I'm not afraid to face them. My general dislike of the Monsantos of the world moved me in that direction.

· chapter two ·

SUFFER NO FOOLS

“You leave home, you learn to deal with the police and government, and you also join the most rebellious metal band on Earth. That’s a potent combination for chaos.”

I didn't speak to my dad for some years after I moved out, although I'd speak to my mom from time to time. He's a very good man, but he's very principled, and stubborn about those principles. I don't fault him for that—in fact, I don't fault him for anything. We're just very different people, and at the time I felt that I didn't want or need any more parenting, while he still considered it his duty to be a parent. In my mind, though, I was now an adult; I didn't have my hand out for his assistance, and I didn't want to hear it from him.

My parents did an excellent job with all the things that they instilled in me over the years. They love me, and we've talked about these events, and I told them that I couldn't be more thankful for what they did for me. Everything contributed to what is. You might ask, *What were you thinking, back then?* Knowing what I know today, I would behave differently if I had to do it all again—but, as I say, all that led to what is today.

In the early nineties, my then-girlfriend and future wife, Gen, told me that it was ridiculous that I didn't have a relationship with my father, so she and my mom conspired to set up a *Treaty Of Wounded Knee*, so to speak. We met, and it was fine. I wasn't angry with my dad; I just had nothing to say to him. I didn't hate him, by any means. We all go through periods when we're running purely on emotions and adrenaline, with one perception. That changes as we learn a little more through life experience, and gain a deeper understanding of truths.

After I moved out, I was searching for something—I guess we'd call it *meaning*. I didn't know what form that meaning would take, but one thing I did know was that I wanted to be in a heavy-metal band. I made it a priority. I practiced playing bass and I enjoyed my improvement.

Soon I met up with some like-minded people at a party.

This chick said to me, 'These guys are in a band.'

The guitar player said, 'Hey, we're looking for a singer. Do you want to try out?'

I did want to. They were called Overlourd. (I still don't know why they spelled it in that medieval way.) It was just one of many starter bands, but we did get as far as writing songs and playing shows. We did a couple of covers, one by the Scorpions, but it was mostly originals. I just sang and wrote lyrics in this band—I didn't play bass—and I enjoyed it, because I was desperately searching for something that I could totally sink my teeth into.

I did other music, too. As time passed, I played with three or four different bands that did a lot of covers. The clubs in Charlotte were all about these A-circuit cover bands, so you learned loads of covers and went in and played three sets a night. That was fun. I enjoyed it because it schooled me a lot in other people's stuff. It really helped me to understand other people's styles; for example, I really got into Iron Maiden from a bass standpoint.

But I was really looking for a band of like-minded people who could take good direction, or were capable of co-writing in a team effort. I still hadn't found them at this point, and I suspect that was because a lot of people don't think the way I do.

There are some musicians that I've met who are extremely well spoken, and for whom I have immediate respect, either by their works or by their demeanor and the way they do things. On the other hand, I've met many with whom l feel I need to remove twenty or twenty-five of my IQ points in order to have a conversation. That's disheartening to me, and I wish it weren't that way.

I wish I had more kindred spirits when it comes to my journey. I feel what motivates me is not necessarily the case for most of the rest of humanity. When I do meet those people, though, I like them a lot, and I gravitate toward them because they're awesome. Those were the people I was trying to find.

Meanwhile, I found a house for rent. It had a room where Overlourd could practice, so one of the guitar players and our soundman and I moved in together. That lasted for a little while, but then the band called it quits because everybody wanted to do different stuff, and I moved to a place just outside Raleigh. I worked on a project there with a couple of guys that I had met. We had odd jobs in landscaping.

I also went to the university in Charlotte for a bit. I took my high-school completion, as well as college courses in the subjects that I was interested in: communications, literature, history, and a few music courses that I only audited, because I wanted to learn about some things and not others.

I did really well at those courses. I was really into debate, and I was the only person like me that had anything to do with it, because everybody else was a law student. I got on the debate team, and oftentimes I would choose the opposite side of my real belief just so I would learn more about the topic, and understand a plausible argument for things being that way. I did really well, although I was so different to everybody else. It was humorous, and I think the Ivy League guys got a kick out of it when I rolled in there with long hair and a different demeanor to them.

I like mental stimulation because I grew up without it. I try every day to have some spontaneous thought or meeting that adds to my portfolio of life experience, otherwise I'll be bored and feel like I've wasted a day.

I wanted to make sure that I finished school—I just wasn't capable of doing it at the previous institutions, because I was ostracized. With college, it was big-boy time; I could go across to a bar and have a beer in between classes. I was in a world of adults, as opposed to a world of a bunch of sheep and rules, because I had my own rules. You either pulled yourself up by the belt loops and did what it was that you wanted to do, or not—and that was a much more comfortable environment and choice for me.

I drifted like this for some time. It wasn't a bad existence. I and whomever I was with always had some kind of low-budget place to live, and some kind of job that was never cozy enough to make us worry about losing it. They were throwaway jobs that gave you enough money to be able to keep on with other things that you valued, like a band.

I was happy in some ways but not in others. I knew what I wanted to do; I just didn't know how to get there. I knew I wanted to be a musician, though. There was no movement on that at all.

Along the way, I passed through so many bands with people who at one time were members of groups that you will have heard of, but for whom something didn't work. None of these bands had much merit, I would say. They were just glances at things. Sometimes they lasted for a month, sometimes a little longer, but they were just stepping-stones.

I worked the door at a rock club for a little while, because I wasn't old enough to be in the bar area. That's where I met Karl Sanders, who is now known for his band Nile. He played in one of the A-circuit bands that appeared at that club fairly regularly. The difference in Karl's case was that they had originals in their set. Those songs were great. It was definitely metal, although it wasn't yet like Nile. It was more like power metal, but with that Egyptian feeling that Nile later had, and they had a great singer who sang in an Italian operatic style.

I used to have long conversations with Karl, who I bonded with. He's a really good guitar player, and there was a connection between us because I'm from North Carolina and he's from South Carolina. That area wasn't what I would call a bastion of open-minded, pioneering, creative metal; in fact, it would be the last area where you'd hear about new bands. I was informed, though, because I'd research stuff through the metal magazines. I used to tell Karl, 'Check this album out,' and play him Metallica's *Ride The Lightning* or whatever.

All the musicians I knew were always saying, 'Dude, we're going to sell everything we own and move out to L.A. and make it,' because at the time there were all these videos of life in Hollywood, like Mötley Crüe's 'Girls, Girls, Girls.' I was tempted, and I considered it, because there was a number of people that I knew who did it, two of whom ended up doing fairly well there. One of them was the bass player from Overlourd.

Everybody else came home bloody and bowed, with their tails between their legs, having had a terrible experience. When I finally got to L.A. and visited the Sunset Strip, it was nothing like it looked in those videos. In fact, it was horrible, and with hindsight I realized that I'd made the right decision.

Conversely, I know a lot of people who live in Los Angeles who are really successful, but I've come to believe that the geographical location of where you choose to live—as long as there's an airport within reasonable proximity—doesn't matter. Live wherever makes you happy, and go where the work is.

Personally, I don't want to live in California, because there are so many things there that are not in agreement with my lifestyle. I can't be me and live there, because I would have to conform to the California life. Yes, they have great weather, I'll give them that, but everything else doesn't work for me.

On the West Coast, people will shake your hand and say, 'Oh, yes, I'm going to help you out,' and what they really mean is, *Go fuck yourself.* Hunting is a problem, cars are a problem because every vehicle has to have all this extra crap on it, and I would have to disown fifty percent of the things that I care about just to live in a place that is too crowded and has shitty, polluted air. It's not worth it.

So here I was in 1982 and '83, looking for a band, and heavy metal was getting heavier by the day, it seemed at the time. 'Extreme metal' as we call it now, or 'power metal' as we called it then—maybe 'black metal' if the band sang about the devil—was coming up through the magazines.

I listened to the original pioneers, Venom, a little bit, but it was too noisy for me, and the quality wasn't there. I did like Mercyful Fate quite a bit, and I got into Bathory later, when their main man, Quorthon, did his Viking-themed albums. Some years later, I actually tried to get him to come out on tour with Morbid Angel, because I had heard through the grapevine that he was trying to get a band together. I also liked Celtic Frost, although their predecessors, Hellhammer, were a bit raw for me. Of the German thrash-metal bands, I liked Destruction best. They defined that sound.

When it came to the very first death-metal bands, I really liked Possessed's first album—even the weird stuff on it that almost sounds like mistakes. The timing was weird, but I couldn't tell if it was deliberate because it was consistent, so I couldn't hear if they were errors or just feeling.

I also loved Voivod, which contradicts what I just said because they were really noisy, but they were so fucking weird. They were a very odd amalgamation—almost punk, almost metal, almost prog, almost lots of things. All my friends hated it—they were like, *What is this crap?* They didn't get it.

I continued to move around a lot and play in bands all over the place. I was in Raleigh for a while, and then I moved back to Charlotte when I was working at the club. I made a lot of quick moves, sometimes every couple of months. I don't think I lived anywhere for longer than six months until I met the guys from Morbid Angel. That was the first band I was in where everybody was as gung-ho and as on point—in terms of discipline and rehearsing for four hours or more per day—as I was. Everything else was hit and miss, with people saying, 'Oh, I don't think I can make it tonight.' The drive wasn't there, which made me bored and angry.

In the bands I played in, we were working on music of an extreme-metal style, I suppose. At the same time, I would argue that Black Sabbath were extreme for their day, so by a process of reasoning we can assume that other things were extreme when they first appeared, although Sabbath didn't have the thorns or quills of death metal, or its subject matter and rasping, atonal vocals.

What was missing for me was music that had passion and a lot of attack—the more the merrier—so I started a label, Goreque Records. It's a random name with no meaning that I came up with. The record-label thing was something I was interested in because I saw other people doing it. I wanted to be involved in some way, not so much for the business of it as for the propagation of the music. I knew what music I liked, and I wanted to build on that as much as possible with the musical revolution that was going on. The idea of pinning a certain type of energy and emotion to good musicianship was important to me.

I had a friend named Mark who had a printing business, and he was also a classical composer and excellent organist. He would do concerts and just kill it, in a Keith Emerson or Rick Wakeman sort of way. He also had a small label with distribution, so I asked him for some pointers about how to get it started, and he gave me some ideas. I was interested in quality metal, so now I just needed a good band to sign to Goreque.

There was a fanzine from Florida that I somehow got my hands on, and of course this was the early days of tape-trading, with no email or internet. I read that Chuck Schuldiner from the band Mantas was from Florida, so I contacted him to see if there was a way to work with him, as they'd never had a bass player on their old demos. I sent him a letter and some photos and a practice tape. I never heard back, so I don't know if he even got the materials. By the time I actually met him, I'd moved down to Florida. Chuck used to come and hang out with us at the beach on weekends.

I knew a singer, Mike, who was originally from Tampa, and one day in 1985 he told me that he'd checked out this cool band and got a tape of theirs called *Scream Forth Blasphemies*.

'What's this?' I said, when he handed me the demo.

'They're called Morbid Angel,' he said.

Man, I heard some really cool stuff on that cassette. It was just a rehearsal tape rather than a well-produced demo, but I liked it, mostly for the guitar playing by a guy who called himself Trey Azagthoth. I wanted to hear more, so I borrowed some money from some friends and visited the Morbid Angel guys down in Florida.

The band was Trey, a guitarist named Richard Brunelle, bassist John Ortega, and drummer/vocalist Mike Browning. I watched them rehearse and I thought the songs were good, so I invited them to come up to a studio in North Carolina and record an album of nine songs. I hired Bill Metoyer, who had worked on Slayer's *Hell Awaits*, to engineer.

They called it *Abominations Of Desolation*. I thought it was more or less adequate. There were some things that weren't quite together, mostly the drums. I could probably have done a better job of helping with some of these things, as I was producing it in a roundabout way, although here that just meant that I made a few suggestions to keep things going and get the parts done right.

One day, after the recording of *Abominations* but before it got released, I was on the phone with Trey, and he said, 'I don't wanna alarm you, but I just parted ways with our drummer and bass player, so it's just me and Richard Brunelle.'

Now, the last thing I was thinking about was actually playing with Morbid Angel. That wasn't even on my radar, and it didn't enter my mind until I got a second call from Trey, who suggested it. I got to thinking about how we could make this work.

My roommate was a drummer who I'd been working with for a long time, so I knew he was good: his name was Wayne Hartsell. I recommended him to Trey and suggested that we all get together. I went down to Florida with a trailer, loaded up Richard, Trey, and their equipment and possessions, and moved them to Charlotte. They could have come up on their own, but I'm the kind of guy who will say, 'Want to do this? Okay, I'll rent a trailer and come and pick you up.'

They came up and stayed in the house that I had a lease on, which was a big place in a rough neighborhood. We practiced and practiced and worked and worked, constantly, Richard, Trey, Wayne, and me.

My friend Mike who had first introduced me to the guys was originally going to do the vocals while I played bass, but he soon quit. I gave vocals a try after he bailed, and we made a couple of rehearsal tapes with me singing, which were so much tighter and more together than anything on *Abominations* that we made a collective decision that it shouldn't be the first thing we released as a band.

We wanted our first release to be the new music we were making, which was undeniably more solid, so we put some of the songs onto a demo tape, to give people a reasonable idea of what we were doing, and started shopping it around Charlotte. We also played a couple of shows, but people weren't ready for it—in that area, at least. Even for fans of heavy metal, that kind of bombastic music didn't exist, so no one knew what to think. For the listeners at the time, we may as well have been singing in Chinese. We were way ahead of the curve.

I received nothing but rejections for the tapes I sent out, but this was still a good time for us. Trey and Richard had moved in with Wayne and me in the house in Charlotte, and we were rehearsing and writing. The four of us got along well, and we were really excited because we were finally doing what we wanted to do—and we were confident about what we were doing. After four years of searching, I felt that this was the band that I had been waiting for.

We spent a lot of time listening to metal, but understand this—we were doing this without trying to follow anyone else. We were doing what we alone were doing. There were bands that we liked, but we didn't want to be anyone other than ourselves.

This wasn't easy to do, for various reasons, not the least of which was lack of support from the metal media of the day, such as it was. For example, there was a period when Chuck Schuldiner moved from Florida to San Francisco to be in a band with the former drummer in DRI, whose name was Eric Brecht. Eric was really fast—he played lightning-fast drums. I really liked it, and so did Trey. However, the principal critic at *Metal Maniacs* magazine just lambasted Chuck and told him that the speed of the music was stupid, and he really got into Chuck's ear. He said the same shit to us—that all this speed stuff was a waste of time, and *if it's faster than Dave Lombardo of Slayer, it's cheating*—all this stuff about cheating on the drums. The idea of cheating didn't compute to me, but the guy didn't like me, or my lyrics, or all the 'silly satanic stuff,' which he also thought was stupid. I was like, *Whatever, dude. Have your opinion. I don't share it.*

This was relevant to us because we started getting some really fast music going on, and finding ways to do blastbeats in a way that I hadn't heard anybody else doing. Trey explained how he wanted to do this to Wayne, and we dissected it and made it perfect. For example, the song 'Thy Kingdom Come' requires a complex beat and very close timing. It took us a while to get our heads around it from a technical point of view; it's almost like a waltz. It's difficult to explain, but we found it, and drilled it, and it sounded like nothing I'd ever heard.

We were reasonably advanced musicians, even at this early stage. I knew what I knew, having played with Wayne in various projects over the years; I could play bass using three fingers on my picking hand, having played along with Steve Harris's bass parts in Iron Maiden for so long. I started with two fingers and added a third because it made sense. Sometimes I used a pick—it depended on the song.

Charlotte obviously wasn't working out for us, so Trey suggested moving back to Florida. 'Why not?' I said, and we hit the road. Once we were down in Daytona Beach, we found a similar house to the one back in Charlotte. It was shitty and so was the neighborhood, and money was always an issue, so we worked in carwashes to put money in our pockets. We'd work for a few hours, then go down to the beach and get laid.

I had a lot of girlfriends and quite a few steady relationships. It didn't hurt that I was in a band, although I didn't need to be in order to get laid. Girls would assume from my appearance that I was a dude in a band. They'd say it *dudeinaband*, as if it were all one word. I had some really great experiences, many of which were very memorable. I'm still friends or acquaintances with some of those women today, even though we've all moved on.

We didn't want jobs that were comfortable or secure, because we knew that we'd lose the hunger for the fight. I knew that to be the case, even at that young age. It was hard work, but we could handle hard work.

By now, we had a band bus, which used to be a school bus, to which we added bunks. We also had a tech who came down to Florida with us. Apart from that guy, there were always people hanging out and helping us where they could. Everything was so organic and relaxed, although we did have the discipline for constant, professional rehearsal. I did the label shopping, and everybody else did their own thing. If a bill was due, everybody kicked in if they were working. Richard handled a lot of that side of it.

Unfortunately, Wayne had a girlfriend who was really demanding and kept lobbying him to come back up to Charlotte—saying, 'Come back up here, you don't have to live in those conditions,' and so on. He was heartsick, too, so one night he just loaded up his stuff and left. I wasn't happy about it, but everyone has to make their own decisions. The guy was a really good drummer, but it was better that it happened when it did rather than right in the middle of a tour, for example. I get the feeling that Wayne thinks he didn't make the best decision, but hindsight is always 20/20. We've remained friends, I'm glad to say.

That's when we got on the phone with Jesse Pintado of the grindcore band Terrorizer, and subsequently Jesse's drummer, Pete Sandoval. I was able to get in touch with Jesse through tape-trading contacts. I asked him if Pete might know any drummers with the particular style and skills that we needed, or even if Pete himself might be interested, and Jesse said that Terrorizer weren't doing anything at the time, and that he was sure Pete would be into it.

We had heard some Terrorizer rehearsal tapes that we had traded, so we were well aware of them, and we liked them. The drums were so fast and clean that we thought it would be awesome to have them in our music, so I called Pete and asked him to play with us. He sold pretty much everything that he had and got on the bus from Los Angeles to Daytona Beach in Florida, ready to join the band. We had never met, only spoken on the phone.

Pete was an interesting guy. He's an athlete with a penchant for high-speed co-ordination. He played soccer when he was a kid in El Salvador. At first, I had problems understanding him, because he had a really thick accent—which he still has—but it was stronger back then, so communications were a little difficult. Anyhow, he got on a Greyhound bus from Los Angeles and came to Tampa with enough money in his pocket to buy a new drum kit when he got here. The bus arrived five hours earlier than scheduled, and when he arrived he didn't have anyone's phone number, so he sat there waiting for us for five hours. We apologized, but that was a bad start.

We found a second-hand double-bass kit, but when we got there he said, 'Why is there two bass drums?'

I asked, 'What do you mean?'

He said, 'I only use one.'

I said, 'Really? I can clearly hear double kick drums in Terrorizer's songs.'

'No, watch!' he said, and he played the kit using only one foot for the bass drum, but at great speed, so it sounded like two drums.

I made some suggestions—for example, that he should lead with his right foot while playing double kick drums—and he was on his way.

Pete worked harder than I have ever seen a person work before. It was totally inspiring. We'd go to work at the car wash and he'd go down to the basement and play drums. We'd come home, hours later, and he'd still be working at it.

We once came home on a summer day when the temperature was ridiculously high. I was walking around the house saying, 'Pete? Pete! Anyone seen Pete?' The basement door wasn't locked, so I went inside and turned the lights on, and there he was, passed out on the floor in a puddle of his own sweat. I said, 'Pete, are you all right?' and he jumped up and said, 'Oh! Dude, I'm sorry, I gotta get back to work.'

It was hotter than Hades down there, and the windows and door were closed. He'd been sitting there in the dark, just working on his double bass drums, for hours on end. This went on for weeks until he was ready to start playing with the band. We rehearsed the songs, and within four months we were on tour, with Pete killing it on double bass drums. I couldn't believe it. It was so inspiring to see someone rise to the occasion like that. That guy is one in a million.

Pete was so determined that he would do it, and he did, with flying colors. I'm so damn proud of him, hunkering down like that for people that he barely knew, in a strange land, because he wasn't an American citizen at that point. Add to that the fact that he was playing new songs on an unfamiliar drum kit, and his achievement is all the more amazing. Without projecting stereotypes, it would have been all too easy for someone from his demographic to join a street gang or take any of a number of unproductive options, but he was a total soldier—he went in and conquered.

Nobody plays like Pete Sandoval. I've played with a lot of drummers, and it's not so much about whether you can play a song a certain way, it's that he has his own kind of groove which is different to anyone else's.

By now, we had sent out a number of packages to record companies, with some songs that ended up on our first album and others which landed on the second. As the singer, lyrics were a big part of my job; Trey wrote the lion's share of the guitar stuff, and the arrangements would be done by us sitting together and banging out the songs as a band.

The songs written prior to me joining obviously already had lyrics. 'Chapel Of Ghouls' was written by Trey, as were 'Evil Spells' and 'Lord Of All Fevers And Plagues.' 'Immortal Rites' and 'Maze Of Torment' were mine, and so were 'Suffocation' and 'Visions From The Darkside.'

The lyrics were inspired by everything that is in my life, and the occult is a part of my life, as we'll see. I was able to tell a supernatural story within a framework, and include references to other things within that story that make it not quite so supernatural.

I felt like the songs on the new demo were tighter, the drums were better, and the whole feel was more solid, but none of the record companies got it. We were a step ahead of what their listening skills had prepared them for.

The companies were the usual suspects at the time, plus a few unusual ones, and every one of them had an opinion.

I gave it a week and then started getting people on the phone.

'So, what did you think of the Morbid Angel demo I sent you?'

I got every imaginable response.

'Ah, well, we think you ought to make some changes.'

'There's too many Angels. Change the name of the band.' This was because there was Angel Witch, the British band; Angel, Rudy Sarzo's old band; and the thrash-metal bands Dark Angel and Death Angel. But I didn't care. I was intolerant of this stuff. I just said, 'Fuck you,' hung up, and then looked for the next one.

'Oh, you know, we think you should slow it down a bit and be more melodic.'

'All right. Fuck you!'

'You know, all this satanic stuff is really passé. You guys should really change your lyrics.'

'Thanks. Fuck you!'

Everybody had some reason why they weren't interested. I was very quick with them. I said, 'So, if we changed the name of the band, are you saying we'd have a contract?'

'Well, I didn't say that ...'

'So you're really not saying anything, then?'

We were so confident in what we were doing that we weren't prepared to listen to any of those suggestions. We had to laugh when we got a response letter from Neat Records in England that said, 'We can only say that Morbid Angel does for music what King Herod did for babysitting.'

We began to look at everything in a really militaristic fashion, like, *Okay, we know what we're doing. We're a band of outlaws, and no one's no is going to thwart us one bit.* In fact, we derived strength from all this negativity and all this *you can't do this* and *this will never work* crap.

We were in touch on a tape-trading level with Mick Harris, the drummer with the English band Napalm Death, and he was really into us. He was pals with Digby Pearson, the owner of Earache Records in Nottingham, and he kept on at Digby about us, constantly saying, 'Morbid Angel! Morbid Angel!' to him. I guess Mick got Dig's interest up to the point where he wanted to sign us, because he offered us a deal for two albums without even seeing us play live.

It wasn't a huge sum of money. The budget for the first album was $5,000, although we went over that a bit. Fortunately, we were super well-rehearsed, and as ready as a novice band could be, so we went into Morrisound Studio in Tampa and knocked out the songs for our first record, which we named *Altars Of Madness*.

Altars started everything that followed. It was the first domino that got pushed over, and the chain is still going. That album is framed and on my wall.

Dig came over for the recording, and Tom Morris produced the album. Morrisound was a respected studio: Savatage had done some work there, as had other bands in the hard rock and metal genres. We didn't go to Morrisound because it was known for death metal, because at the time it wasn't—we went there just because it was a great studio, and it was near where we lived. A lot of bands recorded there after us, once the death-metal wave started growing.

One of the coolest moments on *Altars* is the reversed introduction to 'Immortal Rites,' which happened by mistake. When they were reversing the tape, they left the play head engaged, so we heard the music played backward. Trey said, 'Can we use that on the recording?'

Of course, there was a whole thing about backward masking

back then, with people inserting subliminal messages and so on. I've listened to a lot of things backward to see if any of the words had any weight, and I noticed that any riff that sounded cool played forward was made to sound really interesting and warped when it was played backward. Sometimes we would actually work on riffs and try to make them sound as if they were played backward.

The most rewarding thing was that *Altars* came out and did really well, and all these goddamn labels that had told us this crap about changing the band name and slowing down were all of a sudden like, *Oh, gosh, we need a band like Morbid Angel.* Later, I told some of them, when I met them, 'You guys had a chance to sign us. If you want to push the limits and be visionaries, you've gotta go after bands like us.'

Everything worked on *Altars*. I saw the cover art when I was over in the UK, delivering the masters. The artist, Dan Seagrave, had a number of artworks in progress, and that one was unfinished. I told him I really liked it, and he said, 'Well, it's not done, and I'm thinking of using it somewhere else anyway,' but I said, 'I really want this. What can we do to make this happen?' Dig worked it out with Dan. The image really spoke to the content of the record.

From an American perspective, there's a lot of things about England that make it not like the United States. They drive on the wrong side of the street, they often drink soda without ice, and the food is really bland. I asked myself a pointless, disempowering question when I was preparing to go to England for the first time, which was, *I know they speak English. How different can it be?* I guess I don't even need to explain the answer.

Here in the United States, everything is open twenty-four hours a day, but back then, you had to plan your day around the opening times of various conveniences or you were shit out of luck. You couldn't get a bag of potato chips on a Sunday back then, unless you happened to be on a motorway, where you could stop for some greasy fried bread and mushy peas—and that's going to make everyone else on the bus hate you, because it gives you so much gas.

Understand this. This whole process was like going to war. We'd go into battle, execute our mission, and enjoy success *in spite of* all these naysayers and blockers. Whoever the protagonist was, we came out on top. We'd say, 'This is our battle!' to each other, and use that as internal cheerleading to make us go out and pound it out. There was no doubt whatsoever in our minds; we never second-guessed anything.

We always believed that it was going to turn out the way we wanted it to be. We were at it, at it, at it, and always creating. The more people told us *no* and *stop*, that was just fuel—it was just pouring gas on the fire.

"It took me years of searching to find a band of musicians that matched my own high standards. Once we were together, though, we became unstoppable, because we didn't allow anyone to stop us. You can achieve great things if your will is strong enough. Don't let anyone tell you otherwise."

MAZE OF TORMENT

FROM *ALTARS OF MADNESS*, 1989

Life betrayal, a warping rage
Evil ripping caverns through your mind
Immolation, in blood you've signed your soul away
Sickening life ends but the horror has just begun
Vultures moaning a funeral dirge
Walls await to cradle you and rip your soul apart
Incessant screams echoes through the maze
Insanity approaches, imminent demise
Maze of torment

Stricken from the holy book—deliverance to pain
Effigy of Jesus Christ burning in your mind
Voices cry out to bid you welcome
Locked within the dungeons of darkness—no escape!
Passing through corridors embedded with
Scars of those who have gone before you
And left their marks

Warning comes too late to save you now
Visions of suffering stab from the inside
You pray for death
Mourning does no good as you can only die once
Souls are being raped by the maze
Lost in these halls … endlessly
Maze of torment

A song about suicide. It was happening quite a bit at the time, with people I knew, although this song wasn't about anyone in particular—or me, for that matter. The implication of 'Sickening life ends but the horror has just begun' is that just when you thought your suffering was over, now it gets really bad. Almost a Dante's *Inferno* idea, with the walls surrounding you, ready to rip you apart, and bearing the scars of those who have gone before you.

The idea that 'you can only die once' comes from someone thinking, *If I could only die, and get this over with*, but the answer being, *You've already done that, how did it work out for you?* It's funny, but of course it's very dark, too. I had a lot of fun writing it, because we weren't following any rules. It's still fun to perform, and it has a special spot for me, as all these songs do.

DAMNATION

FROM *ALTARS OF MADNESS*, 1989

Evil minds, grievous sins
Pagan lives have no place for law
Twisted worship exhume the dead
Minds unite for evil cause
Death corrodes the book once strong
Evil lord destroys his foes
Plague has spread throughout the land
Revelations have begun

Call of evil's mastermind
Christians flock to the beast
Burning crosses burn souls
Exterminate the altar of laws
Atrocities of a new Reich
Holy war and holocaust
God weeps and turns his back
The time is right to destroy the world

Damnation
Fill the world with plague
Force of devastation
Tyranny from above

Churning of cities lust so profane
Driving the will to destroy
Crippling powers I'm forced to partake unholy rituals
Crimes of a world barely alive
Melting debauchery
Ashes to ashes, so must I be
Lost in this misery
There's nothing left here for me
I know of no other way
Even death cannot change my ways
I'm first in the line
To hell we shall go

Call of evil's mastermind
Christians flock to the beast
Burning crosses burn souls
The time is right to destroy the world

There are a lot of lyrics here—I wasn't making it easy on myself, by any means. To make it even more difficult for me, Pete's adrenaline levels would make him play these songs faster than normal when we played them live. That would make certain songs hard for me to sing. For example, 'Lord Of All Fevers And Plagues' has lyrics that are really fast, and I need a chance to take a breath at certain points. Above a certain speed, the riff becomes unintelligible, and I have no place to take a breath.

I'm good at professional singing in the sense that I can take a deep breath and get through it, but if Pete sped it up through onstage nerves, I would jokingly say to him, 'Pete, tonight I'm gonna bring the mic back, and you can sing this song.'

He'd say, 'What? I'm not a singer.'

I'd reply, 'Well, if you choose to play it this fast, I can't sing it.'

He'd say, 'Oh, dude—I just get excited.'

Then I'd say, 'Okay then. This is a mid-paced song, so let's measure this. Let's have the fast stuff real fast, the slow stuff real slow, the mid-tempo stuff at mid-tempo.'

Sometimes, Trey would deliberately write riffs knowing full well that Pete was going to speed the shit up live. He wrote the riff with that deliberate intention, phrased so that the picking wouldn't get jumbled up when the tempo went up live.

FALL FROM GRACE

FROM *BLESSED ARE THE SICK*, 1991

Hot wind burns me
Burning as I fall
Cast away
Speechless in the holy way
I survive
The scourge and banishing
To scorching land
I am lord, I take command

Fall from grace

Forgive me not
This knowledge makes me strong
To resurrect
The cities of the damned
All the treasures of Sodom
Now belong to me—celebrate
Fallen angels take my hand

Fall from grace

Whores long for my flesh
And my desire
Lust anointing me now
Consume my soul

I writhe in the flesh and the sins of hell
I am Belial
I bend my knee not but for my selfish desire

I brought this song back into the set recently because it hadn't been played for a period of time in the years of my absence. I absolutely love it—I wouldn't play it if I didn't. It's very passionate, because the song is pretty much my interpretation of Jean Delville's artwork for the album.

In the song, the angel falls from above, but falling is not a bad thing here: it means that we are taking what we are led to believe is bad and turning it into a sense of freedom and liberation.

chapter three

THE MAZE OPENS

"How do you deal with success and retain your humanity? Furthermore, how do you do this with the cops of the world hating you?"

Across my career, I've dealt with many obstacles, great and small. People have often tried to persuade or derail me from the path I've chosen, as people tend to do. They've never succeeded, but it's been amusing to watch them try.

Given that we were Morbid Angel, a death-metal band with occult lyrics, we always attracted adversaries wherever we went. Fortunately, we were made of tough stuff. No one else rolled the way we did. We were a platoon. We viewed our operation very much in military terms and created names for each other accordingly, so Pete Sandoval was nicknamed Commando, because he always wore combat fatigues, and Trey Azagthoth became Treypone, after Sergeant Apone in the *Aliens* movie. We had our dog, Butcher, with us, too—we were like the death-metal Partridge Family.

It wasn't just that our music was so left field: everything about us was from left field, compared to the way that most people lived their lives. We were a rogue outfit who would roll into New York or wherever, and people would look at us and wonder what the hell we were doing.

A lot of tour dates came after *Altars*; we got busy and played a lot, traveling overseas quite a bit through Mexico, Brazil, and the rest of South America. We played in Europe quite a bit, too. We stayed on the road as much as made sense. I have an old passport with stamps in it from countries that don't exist any more, such as East Germany, Czechoslovakia, and Yugoslavia. The lines have been redrawn since then.

We all had ways of preparing ourselves to go onstage. Trey would cut his arms and chest with a razor blade, leading to the release of what he called the *Blood of Kingu*—an occult practice in which bloodletting leads to a higher plane of consciousness. I didn't do it myself. Pete tried it once but he cut himself too deeply and fainted. He cut a deep cross into his arm. You couldn't make this shit up.

It got surreal—and worse than surreal—at times, largely because we had our own way of doing things, let's say, as guys from Florida. Our first American tour in late 1988 was the perfect storm. As I said earlier, we had purchased an old school bus from the school board in North Carolina, because we couldn't afford to hire a real tour bus. We pulled out most of the seating up front, put in some sleeping areas, and cordoned off an area in the back for equipment. It was personalized with a license plate that said 'Morbid' on it, and we added a bunch of stickers on the back windows, one of which said *Fuck the PMRC*.

You may remember the PMRC: the Parents' Music Resource Center, an organization headed by Tipper Gore, the wife of Bill Clinton's future vice president, Al Gore. Back in the eighties, they lobbied the recording industry to put warning stickers on CDs if the songs had explicit lyrics. As musicians, we hated the PMRC, so we attached that sticker to our bus, as well as a whole bunch of others that were basically designed to provoke people.

Needless to say, this wasn't received well by various law-enforcement officers, or by certain members of the public. I remember on one occasion we were driving through rural Kentucky and we stopped at a truck stop. We'd just gotten our very first royalty check for *Altars Of Madness*, and as a result we all had several thousand dollars in our pockets. You can imagine the locals' reaction: we were essentially a bunch of long-haired Neanderthals, and we all had a load of cash, so the staff of the truck stop assumed we were drug dealers.

It was profiling, of course, but we were in a rural area, where people thought what they'd been trained to think. They called the police after we left and suggested that they check us out, so we were pulled over again a few miles down the road. The cops said they were going to search the bus, even though I told them that they had no probable cause to do so. In addition, they had a police dog that they wanted to sniff around for drugs, but Butcher wasn't about to let their dog do any such thing, because the bus was *his* home.

Butcher was very formidable, but the police insisted on proceeding with the search, even after I pointed out that our dog didn't want their dog on the bus. They told me, 'You'd better get ahold of your dog, or we're gonna shoot him,' so to move things along we harnessed Butcher up and took him out of the bus which was difficult, because he was target-locked on the police dog, ready to kill him if he could. I had to walk him quite a way away and sit down with him in order to distract him from the other animal.

In the meantime, the police searched the bus and asked why we had so much money. We gave them a smartass answer: that we worked for a living. They replied that we had an unusually large amount of cash on us, so we explained that, for us, it wasn't an unusually large sum of money because our royalty checks only came in twice a year. In the end, they detained us for forty-five minutes and went on their way.

It didn't stop there. We were Southern guys, so we always had guns with us. But we were also young and inexperienced, so we didn't do our due diligence about what the various gun laws are in different states. To buy a gun in Florida in those days, you simply had to be of a certain age and present a driver's license showing that you were a resident of the state, and then you could buy whatever you wanted. You didn't need a permit. But that's not the case everywhere, as we soon found out.

One night in New Jersey, we spent the night sleeping in a rest stop on the side of the highway. The following morning, the state highway patrol noticed our bus and pulled us over. Now, we used to burn a lot of incense on the bus because we didn't have air-conditioning, and we had Butcher to add to the aroma, so the smell got pretty rank. When the police officer walked on the bus, he smelled the incense and incorrectly judged that we were smoking marijuana. So he looked in an ashtray, and what did he find? Live shotgun shells.

The cops reckoned that seeing the live shells was probable cause to search the bus, which they did, and so they found our guns. When they asked us if we had a permit for them, we said, 'What do you mean, a permit? We have driver's licenses.' If we'd done the slightest bit of research, we would have understood that a driver's license was not sufficient in New Jersey, but of course we hadn't bothered. Worse, one of the guns was a gift from a fan back in Florida, and when the police ran the numbers on it, they discovered that it had been reported stolen.

To put this in context, all of this took place in October 1988, a week after a documentary had been broadcast on NBC titled *Devil Worship: Exposing Satan's Underground*. It was made by the well-known American TV journalist Geraldo Rivera, and it focused on the activities of certain 'cult' groups. You can imagine the cops' reactions when the next thing they discovered on our bus was a stack of occult books. The night before, we had been in New York

City, where we had stopped at a very famous occult bookstore called the Magickal Childe to stock up on reading material.

Add to this a human skull that we had been given by a fan, and the cops probably thought they'd hit pay dirt. We hadn't asked the fan where the skull came from, because we didn't care enough to ask, but we sure weren't grave robbers. That didn't matter, though: hot on the heels of Geraldo's satanic TV documentary, the fact that we were long-haired metal guys with a ton of occult paraphernalia, weapons, a human skull, and the smell of what they thought was drugs, was more than enough for the police officers. They impounded Butcher, our bus, our band gear, and our guns.

We went to jail for a week, charged with weapons offenses, even though none of us had criminal records. The reality is that we in Morbid Angel were agitators and provokers but not criminals. We never killed anyone or stole anything: it just so happened that we had a stolen gun and a human skull in our possession. What the cops really wanted to know was if we had any cult ties, if we sacrificed people, and so on. They saw all this as 'evidence,' because it was in line with what Geraldo Rivera was discussing. They asked us all these questions that didn't relate to guns; they were asking us about our religious beliefs.

Fortunately, the public defender told them it was ridiculous. We appeared in court as part of a chain gang, and they soon realized that there was nothing criminal going on. They gave us what they call a pretrial intervention, where they were willing not to press charges if we kept our noses clean, almost like a probation period. We had to write them a letter every month attesting to the fact that none of us had gotten into any trouble.

It didn't end there, because the New Jersey authorities called their counterparts in our home state in order to make a bunch of problems for us. When we got back to the house we were renting, the property manager came in and told us he didn't want us living there any more. The owners were really scared by the stories they'd heard about this satanic heavy-metal band who owned guns and skulls. We probably could have taken them to court for harassment, but we didn't have the means at that point.

As a result, I have an arrest record to this day, although I wasn't convicted of any crime. I don't actually know anybody who has never been arrested; obviously I don't mean for a serious crime, I just mean being pulled over for speeding tickets or whatever.

To this day, my arrest record continues to have repercussions. As recently as 2012, we were not permitted to enter Canada to play some scheduled shows. As we came to the border, the official asked if I'd ever been arrested. I know what to say in that situation, because my attorney told me, 'You were arrested but not convicted, so you don't have to talk about it, because there's nothing on your record.'

However, all the officials see on their computer screens is the fact that you were arrested and what you were arrested for: they don't see the outcome of the arrest. Unfortunately, this particular immigration official had a real chip on her shoulder, and when she asked if I'd ever been arrested, she didn't like my answer, which was that I'd never been convicted of any crime—in Canada, the USA, or any other country. That was the answer that I was instructed to give by my attorney, but she wouldn't accept it.

I said, 'Honestly, ma'am, I have no convictions,' but she wrote down *uncooperative* on the form. We also had people in our touring party who had DUIs, which seems to be a serious felony in Canada, so they turned us right around and said, 'No way.' I'd been to Canada many times before that, so it was very frustrating, and also sad for the Canadian fans and promoters who lost money on the canceled shows.

Looking back, these incidents were just bumps in the road, and they didn't deter Morbid Angel from our overall mission. Our mission was to be *extreme*. The logo we used on our merchandise, *Extreme Music For Extreme People*, was my idea, and it became one of our most successful shirts, especially as the term 'death metal' became hard to define, whereas 'extreme music' was all-encompassing.

Being signed to Earache brought us into close contact with bands whose mission was similar. At the time, the aforementioned Napalm Death were also doing a version of blastbeats, and indeed Digby told me that Mick Harris was the fastest drummer in the world—we got into an argument about it after I picked Mick's drumming apart and told him he was wrong.

The Grindcrusher tour in November 1989 featured Bolt Thrower, Carcass, and us, supporting Napalm Death. After that, Morbid and Napalm went on tour through Europe. I remember those dates being a lot of fun. It's not fun sleeping in a coffin on a tour bus every night, but it's really the only way to get it done. You can sleep in hotels, but by the time you've checked in you have to check out again three hours later, so it's pointless and expensive.

I loved Carcass—they were one of my favorite bands, and they still are. Bolt Thrower were decent people, too, so the whole thing was copacetic, as I recall. We all sounded different, which was the coolest part. We each had our own thing going. These days, you'll have a four-band bill and they'll all sound exactly the same.

All the guys in Carcass were militant vegans. I remember stopping at a corner shop in England and asking what was in a kind of savory turnover I saw there. The guy said, 'This one's veggie and this one's meat.' I said, 'What kind of meat?' and he said, 'Well, it's meat.' He couldn't tell me if it was chicken, or beef, or anything—just meat. And the way he pronounced it was *'smeat*.

That became a band joke for a while: we'd say, 'Is it *smeat* for dinner?' We also couldn't tell how much of the *smeat* was actual meat. It might well contain the flesh of some animal, but we wouldn't know which animal that was, or how much of it was meat. If I were living in England, I might well be a vegetarian, too, because I don't like eating things with unknown ingredients, especially with the mad cow disease scare they had back in the day. The opposite is the case in countries like Germany, where they have very strict rules about what can be in the food.

Having fruit and vegetables—especially organically grown and free of pesticides—as a large part of your diet is healthy. I happen to like meat, but I am opposed to the mistreatment of animals, so, when possible, I govern what I eat and make sure that it's as close to my way of thinking as possible. Vegans take that a step further and are not prepared to have any part of it. I understand that, and I don't disrespect it, but there's a line that gets crossed back and forth from time to time. Still, I'm not going to change their mind and they're not going to change mine.

There are many examples of people who have spent their lives abusing themselves, and some of them have escaped the ordinary consequences of these things, but a lot of people have a lot of health troubles because they've made really poor decisions. That's a choice as well.

Constant stimulation and spontaneity are key to good mental health. I like to plan, but I also like having an amount of momentary chaos in my life, where out of the blue you go do something and see what happens. Sometimes that opens up doors. These ideas were all key to staying sane on these early tours. The tour income was okay; I didn't go out and buy a Ferrari, but it was reasonable. At the time, my attitude was that we were new to this, so as long as we had good shows and food and a place to sleep, I was happy.

The Napalm guys were just a hoot. Mick Harris and I affiliated pretty well because we're both essentially misfits. He encouraged some bad tendencies that I had, and I went along with it because it was so much fun. We'd smash anything up, and I remember running up damage bills for lots and lots of money. Ordinarily, that's not part of who I am, but back then it felt like a lot of fun. One venue had globe-shaped lights all over the place that looked like bunches of grapes made of blown glass. Mick had a baseball bat and kept shouting, 'Dave! What a doss it is!' while he pummeled these things.

I like Mick—we wouldn't have been signed to Earache without him—and the tours we did with Napalm were hilarious, because he's such a comedian. He'd shout 'Weakeners!' and run in and smash things up. He was a destructive motherfucker.

We in Morbid Angel were more mischievous than destructive, although we did have our moments. It got expensive when damage was done and room fittings were smashed. We made a T-shirt design for the tour with Napalm Death that we called the *Smash Team Tour* shirt, with a skull-and-crossbones logo where the crossbones were crossed baseball bats.

There was a lot of debauchery in general: everyone was young, dumb, and full of cum, as they say, and we went in and conquered. A lot of women were involved. I treated them with respect, and I enjoyed their company to the full. I was a connoisseur of the female form, and I took great pride in ensuring they enjoyed their encounters with me as much as I did with them. This was important to me, otherwise I wasn't doing my job. If I'm going into battle, I'm going to make sure that the job gets done properly. I prefer to spend time doing things well, whether it's enjoying a fine meal, experiencing some quality time with a fine woman, or driving a fine automobile. With everything that I like, none of it is casual, so it gets the attention that it deserves.

I have a slightly chauvinist approach, I suppose, but it comes from love—I'm not a pig about it. I'll hold the door open for a lady. Little things like that. I'll show a level of strength and passion. There are differences between us; hormones are powerful things. Women are governed by an emotional sense of logic that men oftentimes are incapable of feeling. It's important not to dismiss it.

I also believe that we think the same things but we place different emphases on them. When it comes to what someone needs, as opposed to what they get, women need to be loved and men need to be respected. We don't really need love, although we enjoy it.

⛧

In 1989, I worked with Terrorizer on their debut album, *World Downfall*, which came out a few months after *Altars Of Madness*. Apparently, Digby had a contract with Terrorizer prior to Pete joining Morbid Angel.

When I went over to deliver the *Altars* masters to Dig, there was a discussion going on about Terrorizer. They said, 'What's up with this Terrorizer thing?' and I told them that there wasn't really a band per se, and that Pete really wanted to do Morbid Angel. Obviously, Pete and Jesse Pintado and their singer, Oscar Garcia, were around, and they had some demos, but it wasn't really a *band*.

Dig told me that he'd signed Terrorizer but that he couldn't get them to record an album, because everybody was so all over the place. I asked him what his budget was and told him that I would orchestrate getting the record done. Pete was already in Florida, so I flew Oscar and Jesse down and played bass myself. We rehearsed all the songs like crazy until every single one of them was down perfectly. We made them as tight as they could possibly be, and then recorded and mixed the album, *World Downfall*, in two days. Scott Burns was the producer.

It was a cool thing. I was never a member of the band, I just played on the record, and a lot of people were really keen on it. It's punk rock with metal-sounding riffs but no solos, and the lyrics are socially conscious. Shortly after the album came out, Jesse joined Napalm Death, so there really was no Terrorizer after that, until they reformed in 2006. We played Terrorizer's song 'Dead Shall Rise' in our set through *Blessed Are The Sick*, because someone had to play the songs—and, after all, half of Morbid Angel had been in Terrorizer. Trey was happy, too, because he liked Terrorizer.

We toured a lot in 1990 and into '91. Believe me, the 1991 European tour was pretty much off the scale, but despite the fun element, I always took the discipline of it very seriously—the sleep schedule, the workout regimen, everything—because I wanted the show to be the best it could be.

On tour, sleeping is your friend, as well as trying to get some workouts and calisthenics in, so I would sleep twice a day, splitting each day into two half-days. I'd arrive at the venue by lunchtime, eat, take a walk through the city, soundcheck, and then sleep for a couple of hours before going onstage. I'd wake up an hour to an hour and a half before the show, go through my stretches and barbells, do some vocal warm-ups, and go do the show.

My thing was that I didn't want to miss out on the day, but I also didn't want the show to be the last thing in my day. I wanted all my energy to go into it, because that hour and forty-five minutes is the whole reason that I'm there. To that end, I tried to stay disciplined and not overindulge in partying.

Of course, touring can be bad for you. When I came off tour in 1992, the eustachian tubes in my ears were all plugged up, so I had to see an ENT specialist. I'd pushed my voice hard because I couldn't hear properly, and in doing so I'd blown my voice out.

I remember when I went to the initial consultation, the doctor checked my neck and said, 'Were you in a car wreck?' I said, 'No, why?'

It turned out that I had irregular muscle development in my neck, which is ordinarily attributed to whiplash. I told him I played in a metal band, but he didn't get it, so I explained that when you get into the music, you do something called headbanging. He said,

'That's not good!' and I said, 'Yes, I can imagine.' The abuse that you put yourself to on tour is brutal, but I think it's worth it.

A lot of the value of touring, for me, comes from the bands that you share a stage with. We toured with a lot of Scandinavian bands over the years, and I found that they generally have a fun sense of humor. I always got along really well with those bands, and the shows were good. We didn't have a policy as such, but often we'd ask for a Scando band to support us, whether it was Entombed or Unleashed or Grave.

Whoever we were on tour with, just being out on the road brings its own share of comedy. I remember waking up on the tour bus one night and needing to use the bathroom, so I got up and walked through the bunk area, and because the roads were rough, there was quite a bit of movement on the bus, which was ordinarily pretty smooth. On the way back to my bunk, the bus hit something big on the road and swayed, and I involuntarily made some sort of exclamation. The timing couldn't have been better: as my mouth was open, my guitar tech's leg rolled out of his bunk, and his big toe went in my mouth. I was totally grossed out. It was horrible. I instantly backed up to the restroom and washed my mouth out. In hindsight, I can laugh about it, but at the time it was traumatic.

Our outfit was rapidly becoming more professional, not least because we acquired management shortly after signing to Earache. I met Gunter Ford in 1989, and he became my first—and, to date, only—manager. He was working with a couple of local bands up in the New Jersey area, where he was from, and we were coming up to play some shows there. It was really low budget, but we could sleep on the bus and take turns driving, so we did okay. Because of tape trading, we had a halfway decent attendance at some of the shows.

Gunter was managing, or at least helping out, these bands, so he got on the phone and we talked. He asked what we were doing and if we had a manager, and I said no. He said he'd like to discuss that, so we talked some more and explained our setup, and how we had divided our royalties for the first record.

He looked at the Earache deal and asked, 'Who negotiated this?' I said I did, and he told me it was a really good deal, with a fair royalty rate. From then on, that side of our business was handled by Gunter. He had a lot of fire and a lot of drive, and with his help we accomplished a lot of things. For example, *Altars* wasn't available in the States—except as an import—until he got a deal going with Relativity.

We recorded our second album, *Blessed Are The Sick*, in early 1991. Dig didn't come over this time, because we had a better idea of what we were doing, so we just did it at Morrisound with Tom Morris. On the new album, my vocals sounded different from song to song, which was deliberate on my part. I wanted to start broadening the tones and have more diverse vocals, because I don't like everything being the same.

Blessed was different from *Altars* in several ways, not least because its theme was somewhat sexual; the cover artwork is very sensual, relating to taking the dark and turning the lights on. I fell in love with that painting. The estate of the artist, Jean Delville, told us that he was smiling from somewhere about the collaboration. I thought that was perfect.

The title of the painting is *Les Trésors De Satan*, or *The Treasures Of Satan*, and it looks at its subject in a wholly positive way. Lucifer is the light-bearer, and it refers to the womb of desire and other satanic elements that are the antithesis of the Christian viewpoint. You may be familiar with the Biblical phrase 'Blessed are the meek, for they shall inherit the earth.' For us, 'Blessed are the sick' equated to 'Blessed are the morbid.' It all translated really well.

The songs were our strongest yet. Lyrically, our sources varied. Trey was into ancient Sumerian mythology; I was into H.P. Lovecraft, whose writings were dreamy, fantastic adaptations of stories such as the Cthulhu mythos and the horrific visualization that you might get from studying these things. We influenced each other. It was always important to me to include some of the things that Trey had been expressing in our conversations. He'd bring up a point that I hadn't considered, so I'd make a point of considering it and include it in the general delivery of the overall message.

Performing was always a thrill for me. I never got stage fright with Morbid Angel, because I enjoyed it so much. The band was so well rehearsed, and the energy of the audience would envelop you. That energy itself is like a drug. I loved the moments when I spoke to the crowd from the stage, just having a good time with people who came to have fun. I enjoy meeting people anyway, so being onstage is just an extension of that.

When we weren't on tour, we had part-time jobs—tree work and so on—the kind of thing where it wouldn't kill anybody if we weren't there. If I'd wanted a good job with decent money, it wouldn't have been hard for me to get one, but you don't want to get lured into a comfortable situation or you won't want to go on tour. When we went on tour, we'd either put everything we owned into storage, or we'd fill one tiny apartment with our stuff. We'd be gone for months, so why pay bills on a place that we weren't staying in?

All these things evolved. I moved in with a girlfriend; Trey had somewhere; Richard and Pete shared an apartment. Things were getting better, but it was still a battle and a lot of hard work. I wasn't surprised that *Blessed* was popular, because I knew it was going to be. The reaction after it did well from all these naysayers who now wanted to be on board gave me a lot of personal satisfaction. Our plan had worked. That was the way we approached things from then on out. It was us as the Florida wrecking crew who did things our way, without being too concerned about how other people saw things. We didn't care what other bands did; we just cared about what we did. That was the prevalent attitude from all of us.

For us, acceptance was a gradual thing, helped by the rise of extreme metal in general. All of a sudden, there was this tidal wave of really intense music coming out, and reactions to it in the media varied drastically. Sometimes, people fear that which they don't know; maybe the music was unsettling to them—and I'll be the first to admit that extreme music is an acquired taste. It's not easy listening. The average person has to grow into it. Some people are angry, so they like music that sounds angry. We certainly had a lot of those people among our fans.

I saw different publications that were not just anti Morbid Angel but anti anything that was beyond the status quo. At a certain point, though, they had to get some writers who understood the music and were fans of it, because otherwise they were going to lose readership.

The old guard of writers would have squashed us with their words if they could have, but they couldn't afford to be seen as old hat.

It was interesting to see this happen, after fighting battles all my life. Essentially, our army of fans took over the fight for us, so we didn't personally have to get involved in the fray. A whole horde of people out there were happy to write letters to editors on our behalf because they were connected to us now.

Not that it was all plain sailing, of course. The first reaction that I heard to *Blessed* was that we'd slowed down, simply because of the beginning of 'Fall From Grace' and the entirety of 'Blessed Are The Sick.' But the fast stuff on that record is faster than anything on *Altars*. People heard one riff and simply assumed we'd slowed down, but we hadn't. You could take a metronome and hold it up against any of those parts, and you'd soon realize that that comment held no weight at all.

What's more, if what's important to a person is that music is fast, that person is not even scratching the surface of our art. It's a rudimentary, kindergarten way of looking at it. A British magazine called *Terrorizer* once wrote that speed was just one of the weapons in Morbid Angel's arsenal, and that was well stated. People always look for something to complain about, rather than something to be positive about. Personally, I start any analysis with the things that I like.

Earache also issued *Abominations Of Desolation* in 1991, which had never been released before then. This was done in an attempt to quell the tide of *Abominations* bootlegs that we'd seen. People were taking a cassette and printing vinyl off of it, and it sounded terrible. I discussed it with Trey, and suggested that as it was just a historical piece at this point, and it was being bootlegged, at least we should allow people to get a proper-quality copy with the right fidelity. He agreed, so we gave it to Earache as a one-off. It worked out well. There is some magic in that record, I think. It's really interesting stuff, and I'm glad that it came out officially.

Blessed helped us along our way, and as we played the first few shows of the subsequent tours, there was evident growth. We could see it. Our profile was on the incline in a very noticeable and tangible way. We were playing bigger venues to bigger crowds and finally getting proper credit with the magazines.

I quit smoking around this time. The habit had not been helpful to me at all; I'd had problems with insufficient stamina with my diaphragm, which I'd applied more on the vocals on the second album. It was good that I quit, because I'd been a heavy smoker: after all, I was from a tobacco state, where farms were everywhere and cigarettes were a dollar for two packs.

I don't play *Altars* and *Blessed* every day, because obviously I know them inside out, but when I do it's with period-correct fondness, which means that I look back at how I felt at that exact time.

Each record is part of the portfolio, recorded at different times, with different emotions. There are some parallels in the song themes, although I express emotions in different ways. Some of it is more supernatural, some of it is more immediate—but it's all coming from the same place. Beyond the things that initially inspired me, a lot of it came to me simply by being inspired by life and seeing things around. It was my own brand of commentary.

If I went in to record them again today, in particular *Altars Of Madness*, the production would be very different, because we would have greater experience of recording—but I'm proud of those albums. I hear things on them that I would like to have addressed, but why do it now? It's an honest representation of where we were at those moments in time. It's like a tattoo; you can do a cover-up, but part of its function is as a historical record of where you were at a certain time.

To that end, I wouldn't want to change anything, although of course if we made the same records now, there would be some modernization. Not improvements, necessarily. I would have made some of the slow stuff slower and the fast stuff faster, just to make the dynamics a little stronger. But ask James Hetfield how he feels about the sounds on Metallica's first album compared to their later recordings with Bob Rock—there's no comparison.

I recently saw a video on YouTube from a show that we did in Brazil, and I thought, *Those early songs were really cool.* Sometimes, it's only by moving away from things that you can look back and realize how good those things were.

"With Blessed Are The Sick we were finally starting to realize the fruits of our labors. When you work really hard and you see something come to fruition that you created, that is one of the sweetest rewards ever."

BRAINSTORM

FROM *BLESSED ARE THE SICK*, 1991

Gods transform me
The storm will cleanse me
Civilized I shall not be
By this holy strain of laws

I fall below the earth
I smell the ancients' breath
The fiends encircle me
They speak my name in tongues

For I'm no human now
I burn the ways conform
The gods are pleased with me
They speak my name in tongues

I am the seer
I know the texts divine
Thunder words
Demons race into my eyes

Azazel
Lend to me your wings of twelve
I shall fly into the storm
I, son of fire, in anger become
The lightning bolts that strike the earth

This song is twisty: it goes between the upbeat and the downbeat from the intro to the chorus, and again at intervals throughout the song. It's almost like the riff reverses itself as a result, so I remember thinking, *This song is either a tongue-twister or a brainstorm.* The latter can simply mean a gathering of ideas, but I chose to use the *storm* part of it literally. A lot of my writing is about transformation, mostly profound mental transformation, with added horror and occult aspects for entertainment value, and 'Brainstorm' is a great example of this.

REBEL LANDS

FROM *BLESSED ARE THE SICK*, 1991

War-kills on the land
Blood-saturates
Hallowed ground
To which my fathers fell
Rebel souls
Buried deep beneath
This hallowed ground
Land of my ancestry
Drink the blood
Rebel lands rise again

War-death lingering
Blood rivers flow
In sacrifice

Unholy war
Implored from below
No peace as
rebel lands rise

Quaking below my feet
Mortals shall suffer defeat
Forgotten evils below
Rejoice as the blood flows

We might have played this song live two or three times: it's actually a really strange song. It took me a minute to get it, because the riffing is very strange. Trey came up with the title, which was good, because the way the song moved had made me a little stuck. I asked him where he saw the song going, and he explained how certain parts worked—and, once he suggested the title, I had it down. Done. I had simply been unable to see the forest for the trees, so to speak.

Trey and I are very different people. Differences can be either strengths or hindrances, but we always tried to work together as closely as possible. If I ever had a question, I would always reach out, because it was important for me to amalgamate my ideas with others'.

I was inspired here by the Mesopotamian era, going back as far as the Sumerian period and the religions that inspired H.P. Lovecraft's *Necronomicon*. The people of Mesopotamia had their own religion on which Lovecraft's horror and occult writings were based, although in a much more fantastical way. The *Necronomicon*'s authenticity may be dubious, but it's based on an actual religion and a real historical period with its own circumstances; even an old wives' tale has some modicum of truth in it, just as any stereotype has some truth in it. That's what keeps it alive forever, even though the story itself changes through translation over the millennia. There remains something for you to dig your teeth into and use for art.

I was a real Lovecraft junkie. He had a particular style that always left you hanging; there was never any glorious resolution or happy-ever-after, which was one of the things I loved about it. If you allow yourself to be pulled into his world, it's like a carnival or rollercoaster ride: you have to give in to it, let your boundaries down, and try to walk the path with him. He plants seeds and lets your imagination take over without defining things, because undefined—and, indeed, unmentionable—things are very powerful in this world that wants to quantify and qualify everything. Those who imagine and dream, and turn those dreams concrete, go on to great things.

DAY OF SUFFERING

FROM *BLESSED ARE THE SICK*, 1991

A call to take your hand
For I'm at one with the dark
How dare you come with me
And again you must die

So ancient curse known to me
Behold the powers I unleash
Upon your throne
Know my words, feel my hate descend

Lord of light
I will swarm against you now
Gods perverse
Wicked at my side
Misery
Thorns to lance your every word
Nazarene
Now I crown you king in pain

Suffer!

This is a short song—an in-and-out burner. It's a dark, attacking rebuke against being called to do something and saying *go fuck yourself* in response. I mention Lucifer, the Lord of Light, here, although many Christians would consider him the Lord of Darkness, despite the meaning of his name.

Religion has been really good over the years at planting holidays on top of other holidays that people were already celebrating, and then renaming and basically hijacking them. But rather than letting something be hijacked, you can go right back and correct the inaccuracies, as it were.

• chapter four •

HEAL THE SOUL

"You work. You sleep. You work. You sleep again. And, along the way, you forget to evolve. Here's an object lesson in how to reach a breaking point and survive."

Life continued to evolve for me, in and out of the band.

I met Gen after she had graduated from premed school in the early Nineties: her band, Genitorturers, had been going since 1986. There was a Napalm Death and Godflesh show in Tampa that night, but I really didn't feel like going out; a friend of mine persuaded me to come and hang out. Gen had recently become single, and her friends had talked her into going to the show. It's funny to think that neither of us had planned to go out that night.

She was a very attractive lady; in fact, I was entranced by her. I made my way over to talk to her, and we got along really well. She was very bright, very talented, and very funny, and we started seeing each other after that.

I was preparing to go on tour at the time, so essentially I didn't have a place to live because I was couch surfing. When I did have an apartment in Tampa, or Gen had her place in Orlando, I would stay there. We ended up buying a house together in 1993.

Drugs reared their head in the life of Morbid Angel at this point. Personally, I neither need nor want drugs in my life, but I've certainly tried many of them. Fortunately, I don't have an addictive personality, but I did smoke a lot of pot and take a lot of acid. The latter of those made the most intellectual impact on me; it had interested me since I'd learned about the Woodstock generation as a kid. It enables the user to build different pathways toward enlightenment in the brain, although I've learned to do that without needing to take the drug itself, which can have unpleasant side effects, especially for long-term users.

To make acid work, you need to know how to govern your mood; I've helped friends through very scary trips before. I was fortunate enough to see Timothy Leary speak, and to talk with him; he had incredible energy and was quite a character. He was intriguing—a rocket scientist on a different kind of spaceship.

I rarely drank before going onstage, apart from a couple of Red Bulls, perhaps. We had alcohol on the rider, but it was mostly the crew and me who drank it, and Pete a little bit, but not to excess. Maybe if we had a day off the next day I'd light it up a little bit more, but never to the extent that it would affect the performance. It was the honorable thing, for me.

Occasionally cocaine was around. I recall one particular tour in South America where we had a really grueling schedule. The plan was to fly in, do a show, go back to the hotel, drink a beer, and try to wind down a little bit at three in the morning. The hotel lobby call was at six, because we had to make an international flight by eight. There were several days of this, and we were essentially sleepless.

We arrived in Argentina to do the last show of the South American run, and we wanted to go to the hotel and have a nap, but the promoter said, 'Oh, no, we have press interviews and an in-store signing for you!' He asked if we needed anything, so I suggested that a gram of coke would help, because we were absolutely exhausted. Somehow the word 'gram' didn't translate, though, and he came back with a golf ball–sized rock of cocaine and said, 'Here you are.'

Being so close to the source, the coke was extremely good quality and pure, and pretty soon everything seemed great again. We finished all the interviews, did the in-store, played the show, and headed back to the hotel. I sat in my room and looked at this boulder of coke in front of me, and—like a true American—said to the rest of the band, 'Well, we can't just throw it away.'

'Yes, that would be wasteful,' the others said, and we chopped out line after line. Soon, those of us who had taken part were beside ourselves. I literally couldn't get any higher. It wasn't possible. But I looked at this thing and it didn't even look like we'd made a dent in it. I wasn't a buyer of cocaine, and I would only do it occasionally if it were offered to me, so I'd never seen it in this kind of quantity before. But we didn't have a show the next day, and I didn't really need to get any sleep, so what harm could it do?

We spent the better part of the next six hours consuming as much of the cocaine as possible. I now know what ten out of ten on a scale of being high on coke is, because I reached that point. I looked at it almost from a tourist's standpoint. I would in no way recommend to anyone that they try this, of course, but understanding the pinnacle of the experience was very interesting.

Fortunately, I've had a safe journey through drugs, but I've had a lot of friends who did not survive that journey. I'm sure the readers of this book have had less-than-positive experiences with drugs themselves, or know people who have been there. I explored it, and I have no need to revisit it ever again. As I say, I don't encourage people to do these things; I'm clean and I have been for a long time.

In the case of our guitar player, Richard Brunelle, drugs became a sad story. The reason for his leaving the band was substance abuse. In fact, he did jail time for it. We were in rehearsal, working on our next album, *Covenant,* and I was standing in the middle of the room and not singing, because I wanted to make sure that everything was really tight. My ability to pay attention to every detail of the whole is diminished if I'm adding to the cacophony, so I would spend a lot of time just listening to the interplay. On this occasion, I was listening to two things that were not complementing each other. Of course, I was going to comment on that, because I'm a perfectionist.

'Dude, what's wrong? Trey, can you show him that part again?'

So Richard was fired from the band. He really was a good guy, and we tried and tried to help him, but to no avail. As a result, Trey played all the guitar parts on *Covenant*. Richard died in 2019 at the age of fifty-five; when I heard the sad news, I raised a glass to the good times we shared.

The story behind *Covenant*, which I'm told is the biggest-selling death-metal album ever released, is an interesting one, because it reflects a major change in the music industry.

When it came to the album titles, if recollection serves me correctly, I think it wasn't immediately our plan to follow alphabetical order. That didn't happen until the realization of it came with *Covenant*. *Altars Of Madness* was Trey's title, *Blessed Are The Sick* was mine, *Covenant* was mine, and I think Erik Rutan came up with *Domination*.

Our deal was up with Earache after *Blessed Are The Sick*, but Digby Pearson had had an offer from the major label Columbia. They wanted to distribute the bigger bands from Earache—in other words, Napalm Death, Carcass, and us. Dig didn't have the power to negotiate on our behalf because his contract with us was up, and he didn't have the ability to do the deal with Columbia based on Morbid Angel.

So Gunter said to Dig, 'Okay, we'll re-sign with you, but for the UK and Europe only.' He then got us the deal with Giant/Warners in the States, as well as separate deals in Japan and Australia. We were the first extreme-metal band signed to a major label, which felt very cool.

Gunter got in there and rolled up his sleeves, and I really give him full credit for making the deal happen. He carved up territories for us, which meant that if one area didn't do well, it wouldn't affect the others, and it also gave us direct relationships with all the different regional teams, which kept us involved and strengthened our position in those areas. It really helped us with the building of the band.

The budget for the two albums we signed with Giant for was big, but the terms of the deal were considerably different to those that we were accustomed to. We weighed it out, and on the plus side, we retained our publishing; on the downside, the royalty rate per unit was considerably lower than we were used to from Earache, but doors were being opened to greater opportunities, which outweighed the money we weren't collecting.

We were subsequently proven correct in this analysis. The tours were much bigger, and we now had a huge machine behind us, with big budgets for videos. We did two videos for singles from *Covenant*—'Rapture' and 'God Of Emptiness'—both of which were played *ad nauseam*, to the point where even *Beavis & Butt-Head* picked up on them.

We didn't lobby for that, but a lot of fans were upset because it is a spoof cartoon TV show, and the characters said, 'What's that—a bear?' when I roared. I remember fans would write me and say,

'Man, it fucking sucks that *Beavis & Butt-Head* are making fun of you'—but lo and behold, every time they would make fun of me, there was a check in the mailbox. It was great exposure, and those things continue to be rerun to this day.

'God Of Emptiness' was a big crossover song for us. It was the first time I'd sung cleanly in a Morbid Angel song. I've always explained this by saying that just as there were big differences between *Altars* and *Blessed*, there were big differences between *Blessed* and *Covenant*. Each record increased the palette, and it didn't hone in on anything except diversity. We chose different textures, different feelings, and different sounds. (I have since learned that the band Korn later covered 'God Of Emptiness' but didn't release it. I'd be interested to hear their take on it.)

We recorded *Covenant* at Morrisound and mixed it at Sweet Silence in Copenhagen with Flemming Rasmussen, who had recorded three Metallica albums over there. Trey and I went over for the mix.

Flemming is a good guy; he's smart. He came over and oversaw the recording of the drums, because he wanted them recorded a certain way. He sat with us in rehearsal a bit, and then we went into the studio for the initial setup and the actual recording of the drums. This was all done to two-inch tape, because this was before Pro Tools, so he spent plenty of time cutting slices out of tape.

For the beginning of the *Covenant* tour, we got Erik Rutan in the band. He was playing in Ripping Corpse, another band under Gunter's wing, and he was a really good guitar player, as well as a real hothead; he was a bit younger than we were, and he didn't have our experience.

When he came in, there was a little bit of machismo at first: I don't recall the details, but I think he wanted to bring a girl on tour. We didn't think it was a good idea, which made him really angry, to the point where he wanted to get physical about it. In fact, we got Richard back for a brief part of the tour before Erik returned, having chilled out a bit. I'm glad we worked it out, because Erik's contributions to the next album, *Domination*, were very appropriate. I have nothing but respect for Erik—he's a great guy and a good friend of mine.

We toured a lot at this point. The number of European bands I've played with, and with whom I've built a good relationship, is large, and I look back fondly on all of them. We toured with a lot of bands, some more than once, and I've enjoyed sharing both stage time and offstage time with them—Sadus, Entombed, Unleashed, Carcass, Napalm Death, and Bolt Thrower among them.

We played shows with the other Florida death-metal bands—Atheist, Deicide, and Obituary, among others—but not full tours, at least not while I was with Morbid Angel. Now and then we'd put together a Tampa show with all those guys, and I enjoyed doing them, although it seemed that sometimes there was an underlying air of competition when it came down to where bands were on the bill. I always said, 'I don't care, I'll open the show.' It didn't matter to me, but it seemed like it was a little more important to others. They were good shows.

We didn't really play with the older thrash-metal bands, because they were considered to be a different subgenre of metal, although we played the Sweden Rock festival one year with Joan Jett, The Cult, Judas Priest, and loads of other bands that you wouldn't necessarily associate with us. It was typical of the diverse nature of those European festivals.

✡

When we signed to a major label, some people predicted that we would sell out and play slower music that was less heavy than before. In reality, our faster stuff got faster. Again, people's first inclination is to find something negative, fixate on it, and complain about it.

I had a conversation about this once with the founder of Dean Guitars, Elliott Rubinson, who was a close friend of mine, when we were sitting near the outdoor smoking area at his company headquarters. He was talking about the negativity of cigarette smokers, which had never occurred to me before.

I said, 'I agree that it's a filthy habit, but what do you mean by negativity?'

He replied, 'Do you think they're out there enjoying themselves and saying, *What a beautiful day it is! I love my job at Dean Guitars. That Elliott Rubinson is a really nice guy*. No, they're commiserating, saying, *That Elliott guy, I told him to go fuck himself!*'

This had never dawned on me before, but he was absolutely right. Smoking turns into a negative-fest, if you will. I thought to myself, *Is he right?* I went to talk to one of the smokers. I said, 'How are you doing?' The guy said, 'Oh man!' and started grumbling.

What was most concerning was that I recognized this grumbling in myself. It was the same way that I used to start my day—as a way into attacking another day in Morbid Angel.

Let me explain, because this was the start of an important process for me.

The period around the *Covenant* album was a good one. Things were working out, and I was in the moment, appreciating that. However, I was starting to ask myself where I was getting my angst from. To be the frontman of a band like Morbid Angel, you need to treat each gig as a battle—but it's not as much of a battle when you're making a lot of money, because you have really nice buses, and better tours, and the other good things that come with hard work. I didn't want to lose the fight at that point, so I was finding things to be upset about, because that negative energy fueled me, or at least I allowed it to fuel me.

I went too far with it, unfortunately. I would deliberately focus on things that were annoying to me, so that I would feel angst, because that would fuel me to go out and attack onstage. It got to a point where it started rubbing some folks the wrong way.

If I saw something as being stupid, I would just say it. I would call it out in a rude, dismissive fashion. For example, if I walked into a dressing room and the sandwiches didn't look good, I'd take the tray and throw it out in the hallway, rather than simply ask for them to be replaced. My tolerance was zero for just about anything. To me, this was about keeping my edge, at a point when there were no more Christian groups to lambast, and there was no real enemy who was against us.

Essentially, I was being a dick. But I didn't have too much time to spend thinking about this just yet. We toured like crazy after *Covenant* came out in 1993; we were always out there, solidly on tour for two or two-and-a-half years per record cycle. We'd do headline runs, support runs, festivals; we were open to anything. The more people that we had the opportunity to convert, the happier we were. I had no problem opening or closing for anybody, because we weren't in competition with anyone, besides ourselves.

Not long afterward, we did something completely new when we collaborated on an EP with the Slovenian band Laibach, who remixed some of our songs. I loved Laibach; I understood what they were doing and thought it was so brilliant. They had formed under a totalitarian government in a country where pop music was forbidden, so they literally started a music and art project that reflected exactly what their existence was. Their government didn't know how to deal with them, because it looked as though it was supportive of exactly what it was they were trying to do. It was an artistic take on what their lives sounded like, living where they did.

They're not what they appear to be at all. Very cool guys, very nice—but very pure artists. Their influence is obvious on the more recent band Rammstein, whose production is amazing, but who would not exist without Laibach. I do admire Rammstein, though: for that band to come over to the States and sing only in German, and in doing so sell out big hockey arenas, is incredible.

We were fans of Laibach, so we mentioned to Dig that it would be cool if we could get some kind of collaboration going. They weren't really familiar with us, having never been approached by something that was not of their world before, but somehow Gunter and Digby got it worked out, and the *Laibach Re-Mixes* EP was released in 1994. A lot of people were like, 'Why would you do that?' and our reply was, 'Because we're Morbid Angel, and we do things differently.' That's the name of the game, isn't it?

We had signed to Giant for one album plus an option, and

they exercised that option, so now we were into recording the next album, *Domination*. It was the first record we made with Erik where he contributed in the songwriting.

When *Domination* came around, Giant had an A&R guy that wanted to work with us. I remember Gunter getting on the phone and telling this guy, 'You're not allowed to go down to the studio. When the record is ready for you to hear, you'll hear it.' He really didn't want the label people to get involved.

Our producer this time was the late Bill Kennedy, who had done a lot of stuff—he had worked with Glenn Danzig, Trent Reznor, Black Sabbath. I liked Bill. He was really gruff, and a chain smoker. They had to get an air-filtration system into Morrisound, because he got angry about having to go outside to smoke. He was really deeply into the music.

At one point, Gunter phoned Bill up and said, 'What do you think?' and Bill told him, 'We have a hit called "Where The Slime Live."'

Now, that's a catchy song—although we never thought about writing a song for that purpose. Trey and I wrote it together. It goes down really well live, and it's a fun song to play. The vocals were recorded with an effect called a watery flange, which reminded me of hot volcanic springs with boiling mud flats. We did two videos for that song; the first one was shot too dark, so we went in a completely different direction and reshot the entire video.

Domination goes in a lot of different directions because it's more fun that way. Playing constantly on ten is not effective: it's best sometimes to drop to an intensity level of four or five, because from four or five you can go back up to ten. It's a very orchestral album.

I like albums that are different-sounding, with different guitars and drums and phrasing; that makes it more of a rollercoaster ride. The intros and instrumental parts between songs became one of our signatures; there wasn't another band of our genre doing that at the time, although there are a lot of them now.

These parts were a reflection of the music we listened to outside the band—in particular, classical music. We liked the feeling of that music, and we wanted to make that a part of the emotions that we were presenting, although not necessarily in that exact style. It was more of a nod in the direction of beauty and ugliness, coalescing into the pleasures of the flesh.

We sold a lot of records at this point, although I didn't make a lot of money—at least initially—because the budgets were so high. But it opened up a whole bunch of doors for us, for big tours and so on. The videos that Giant paid a lot of money for were MTV sensations. That was especially cool because I don't think we would have had the ability to get on screen without the label going, 'Play this, MTV!' They were among the top videos for that year on *Headbangers Ball*; they got so many requests and they went viral.

The director was a really artistic, visionary kind of guy. The sets that his team built, and the locations that we chose, were really well done. They were expensive, too, but Giant was shoving money at us. *You need tour support? No problem.* They wanted to give us as much as possible, because it was all just going to come out of our royalties anyway.

In this business, you basically get paid twice a year. You get large chunks of money, depending on how much touring you do, so it looks like you have a lot, but you have to think ahead and plan for the long term. I'm not complaining; we did things in a smart way, and I'm fortunate that I was able to appreciate the fruits of our hard work.

By and large, the tours after *Domination* went smoothly. There were always upsets with bus breakdowns and mishaps along the way, some of which were pretty severe. We had an accident on the same highway between Oslo and Stockholm where Cliff Burton had died, in the same general proximity. It wasn't the bus but the equipment truck, so all of our equipment was gone. We grabbed a couple of guitars and headed for the venue, but the backline they had quickly assembled wasn't ready, so we ended up not playing a sold-out show. The promoter said, 'It's okay, we'll bring you back,' but the kids were angry; they didn't understand why we couldn't play. We weren't happy with any of the crew, or the tour manager, so we didn't play. It was not good.

Apart from that, we had our routine down pretty well. For example, Trey doesn't like to be in the light when he's performing, because he's a reclusive kind of guy, and if there's a light on him, he moves his stuff in order to purposefully stay out of it. There's light on me, though, because I'm doing my job. I want the front of the stage lit up like a Christmas tree. I don't care if the lights are in my eyes—I want everyone to see what they bought a ticket to see. We should all be visible, in my view, because you're either a performer or you're not. It makes sense. If you give a good interview, people will want to interview you; if you take a good photo, people will want to photograph you.

Still, I was a lot more hotheaded then than I am now. Like I said earlier, we had this idea that being in Morbid Angel should be like a constant battle. Everything seemed exactly like that—combat—and you don't go into battle holding a cup of tea with your pinkie out. You're amped up, which was something that, in hindsight, was not very helpful to me.

Physical confrontations were not something I enjoyed, but I think everybody is involved in some form of that at some point in their lives, and sometimes there are situations that need to be handled—and, with emotions running high, it seems at the time that that is the best way to handle it.

We were winning all our battles, and I represented that to myself as, *What's wrong here? What's the target? Where's the angst coming from?* We were doing well, getting good crowds and making good money, and I didn't want to relax.

I was searching for something to be angry about. In my own mind, I hadn't yet connected some of the dots that I'm connecting for you now. In my own mind, in order to keep it real—so to speak—and with the idea that combat was part of that, I wanted to feel angst. Rage would enable me to deliver that onstage successfully, as I saw it, and I'm not good at faking things; if something doesn't feel real, it doesn't work for me. I need to be authentic.

In my defense, I was required to endure an arduous stage performance every night. No matter the subtleties of the lyrics and the emotions and the messages, I needed to be pumped up—and, for me, rage and anger were a way to do that. When you're playing large, packed houses on big tours, and money's not an object, what is there to be angry about, other than that which you seek out to focus on?

For this reason I would intentionally make myself angry, which of course made me hard to stomach at times. For lack of a better word, I behaved like a diva. I had a bad attitude, and that was amplified by my surroundings. I was not violent toward people in a physical sense, but verbally I was. If I was doing an interview with the press and I didn't like the interviewer or I was asked what I regarded as a stupid question, I would attack them and the conversation would quickly go south.

If I got annoyed, I wasn't going to put the brakes on. People did ask some genuinely stupid questions, and I gave them answers that were even more stupid. Or I might pull them in a direction that I thought would be as annoying to them as the idiocy of their questions was to me.

In the end, this became a problem. We were doing a lot of touring, and I had given a couple of negative interviews around the time that we were recording *Covenant*. I don't make excuses, and I take full responsibility for the words that come out of my mouth, but in hindsight I see that my ego was getting away from me. I felt as though I was above it all, and that didn't come from a place of insecurity but from a place of ambivalence.

This strained my relationship with Trey and Gunter a little bit. A breaking point was obviously coming, because me being an asshole got even worse from the *Covenant* tour onward. Pretty much everyone around me told me I should behave better, but I wasn't ready to hear them. Sometimes your ego is not your amigo. I would have dismissed any comment of that nature, in the same way that I would have dismissed any comment made to me.

It was as if I'd found a path, begun rolling on it, and then realized that I didn't have any brakes—so it was like, *Fuck it, let's keep going with no brakes.* Again, hindsight is 20/20, and at the time I was flying on pure adrenaline and emotion, which takes away any logic. I got to the point where I was unhappy, because the man in the mirror didn't like what he saw. There was blowback on others because of the ways that I had chosen to conduct myself.

I remember a time when I thought it was a good idea to go to the gym and do steroids and work out with buddies as part of the rage. Some time later, I was driving one day, and some guy cut me off in traffic. I was so angry that I got out of the car at the next traffic intersection and went to pull the guy out of his car. The rage was so intense that I literally couldn't see. Gen was screaming at me—'What are you doing? This is crazy!'—and fortunately I stopped just short of what I wanted to do, but I felt it. I *totally* felt it. It was part of an overall situation, and in many areas I was still functional, but in other areas I had lost control of myself.

The consequences of some of the ways that I had chosen to act were mounting. These included a downgrading of all my relationships, not just with the band but with agents, promoters, and anyone who was close to me in my personal life. I was coming toward a breaking point prior to the last tour that we did for the *Domination* album.

There was another factor, too. At this point, around 1995, there were a lot more bands doing what would be considered our genre of music, and I remember playing shows where some of the audience reaction wasn't at the level that I was expecting and had come to enjoy. I got really irritated with this one day, so I decided to walk out front during soundcheck and hear what we sounded like. I stood at the mixing board, listening to it, and I thought we sounded great.

I asked a friend what he thought, and he agreed that we sounded crushing, but he added, 'Look at the bands you're touring with.' We used to be the sole band—or one of very few bands—who played music this way, but now we were surrounded by bands whose drummers all wanted to play like Pete. Our impact was lessened as a result.

Then we got into festival season, and some of the festivals that we had previously headlined were now being headed up by a different kind of music—usually from the new crop of New York hardcore bands. I asked myself, *What just happened? Our sales haven't dropped, and our sound is good.* I came to realize that the demographic was changing.

Nu-metal was also on the way in, and death metal had arguably been a trend for a while. I didn't feel that Morbid Angel were trendy, though; we just did what we did and it caught on. There was a wave that became popular, but we had arrived before that wave.

'What's going on?' I'd ask. 'We headlined this festival last year.' The answer would be, 'Well, this new kind of music is really popular now.' I'd listen to it and say, 'This stuff is terrible!' Death metal was now defined differently to the way we originally defined it as Morbid Angel. We included the familiar elements of power and technical proficiency, but the varying speeds and more diverse textures made us more than just a death-metal band.

I used to come home from tours with a whole pile of CDs, because if someone takes the trouble to give me their CD, I'll listen to it. Some of it I liked, and some of it excited me, because I'm a fan of music and I want to like stuff. Often it sounded like a poorer version of something that I, or someone else, had done a decade before. In Morbid Angel, we never, ever listened to another band and said, 'Let's try to sound like that'—ever. We had music that we listened to and liked, sure, but we never went after a sound that was popular.

All this added up to impending doom, as I saw it—and I knew that I needed to make some changes. Trey and I had always talked about how we both liked live records, so we decided to record a live album of our own. We took recording gear on tour and taped multiple shows, and I knew that that was going to be my last tour.

I didn't tell anyone that I was leaving, because I didn't want to add yet another variable to an already complex situation. The last festival I did was at Graspop in Belgium on July 2, 1996. We finished the last song, I said goodnight, I laid the mic down on the stage—and that was it.

So why did I leave? It was a bunch of things that all added to my overall unhappiness, and the way that I was expressing that unhappiness to my bandmates and everyone in my life. I wasn't being the kind of person that I wanted to be around. My ego and attitude meant that I was really out of whack. I told Vanessa Warwick, the TV interviewer at Graspop, that I was quitting Morbid Angel to join Gen's band, Genitorturers, but that wasn't really the case, although I had worked with Gen in the past. I only said that to make it clear that I wasn't retiring from music.

The Morbid Angel live album, *Entangled In Chaos*, was my parting gift, if you will; it was released in 1996, but I didn't get involved in the mix or the release. I had suggested that we do a live record so that I could leave the band with a product that could buy them some time to find a new singer. As I said, I didn't tell the other guys in the band I was leaving, because I didn't want to put an additional black cloud into the mix. One of the guys in the crew knew, but he didn't say anything. The rest of the band found out when they got home.

> ***"My life was totally negative at this point. Why do people look at something and the first thing they try to do is find something that they don't like about it? Why not start with what they like? Once you start bad, it just goes down from there. You could start good and maybe have a few areas to criticize, and then you'd have a balance. If you go immediately toward the negative, it's hard to rebound from that. I didn't know this when I was young, of course—and what you've just read demonstrates that point. Fortunately, better times lay ahead."***

BLESSED ARE THE SICK / LEADING THE RATS

FROM *BLESSED ARE THE SICK*, 1991

Havohej, another me born to serve
To plague and moan
So many years my seed condemned
Not free to soar

Will is yours? So, creator
No intend could shadow
My disease … ever-lusting pain

World of sickness
Blessed are we to taste
This life of sin

My touch is inhumane
Nocturnal beast inside
Is void of light
And empty shall remain

The first word is 'Jehovah' backward. At the time, people would say, 'Oh, if you listen to something backward, is it going to say something different?' so we backward-masked it, just to make it easy for them. Live, I sang it as it sounded on the record.

This song is a parody of the Biblical phrase 'Blessed are the meek,' which basically instructs us toward compassion. I thought of 'Blessed are the sick' as meaning having a sick mind, and the message is essentially that those who think outside the box prevail.

When I look back, I see that I put up with quite a bit of protest from various religious groups. There would be picketing outside shows, and the concerts might get canceled, and there would be news stories about us, but I always found it really entertaining that people would worry so much about our songs.

Looking back on it, and the folly of it all, it was so beneath everybody, myself and those groups included. If you don't like something, just don't buy it, but the protesters never understood that. It reminds me of the 'God Of Emptiness' video, where I'd get paid every time Beavis or Butt-Head said something sarcastic about my vocals. I loved it. Fans would get all angry about it, but I would tell them that I actually wanted more of it. I met the show's creator, Mike Judge, once, and told him how much I appreciated it.

We wanted 'Rapture' to be the first single, so we did a three-song EP in the States of 'Rapture,' 'Pain Divine,' and 'Sworn To The Black.' We kept 'God Of Emptiness' as the ace in the hole, and it worked.

THY KINGDOM COME

FROM *BLESSED ARE THE SICK*, 1991

Restless minds beneath the ground
Through ghostly winds I hear the sound
Crying forth in ancient tongues
Eternal quest of vengeance
From tombs of scorn cadavers rise

Angered fury in their eyes
Solemn rage, a need to kill
Feasting on holy hordes

Evil curse is carried forth zombies rage
Burning holy images in life they were
Forced to hail
Eternal flames have purified their souls
Born again in blasphemy, thy kingdom come

Twisted oath nodebliwith [thy will be done]
Preying on those who seek the cross
Let none be pardoned for their crimes
Feeble race will die
Scripture burns in infamy
Tortured souls have been set free
Taunting he who sits on high
Pray thy kingdom come

Banished from the living
Bodies long decayed
Mass of resurrection

Sepulchers abandoned
Insurgent souls arise
Disseminating evil

Curse of devastation
Implored by hell's command
Darkness rips the land

Morbid priests serenity
Sing praise
Thy kingdom is at hand

This song didn't change much from the demo to the final recorded version. The crux of the story is that people who died, and had been told that there was a certain afterlife waiting for them, had realized on dying that it was all a bunch of gibberish, and so came back out of pure anger, which reanimated them. 'Burning holy images in life they were forced to hail': they're taking their revenge there. It's based on the dark, occult themes that have always been a part of my psyche.

I pretty much knew where I was going with some of the phrasing. There were some areas where I didn't leave myself much room for breath, but I didn't amend it. The sound of an initial *h* is difficult to enunciate strongly because it requires a lot of wind to come out, so to speak. It uses throat more than diaphragm, but I've learned over the years to shape it properly. Any vocalist will understand what I'm talking about here. This is why you do scat vocals over the top of a demo, to see where the vocals fall comfortably. Of course, sometimes they still don't feel comfortable, but you just have to man up and do it.

PAIN DIVINE

FROM *COVENANT*, 1993

Release this fury
Malediction
Cursed existence
Writhing in this life of dissent
Pain for pleasure
Pain for adoration
Pain is to godliness
Bleeding for ecstasy

Pain divine

Locked in vicious
Offer to the sado-gods
Nails driven through my dreams
Bleeding, pain is a god's reward

Gliding through these dungeons
Heightened senses overwhelmed
Hedonistic rupture
Endurance makes one divine

My ex-wife, Gen, introduced me to the work of Roland Loomis, who called himself Fakir Musafar and performed suspensions as part of his mental discipline. He would hang naked from a tree from hooks that were inserted in the flesh of his chest, and in doing so found a connection with Native American spiritualism. Obviously the pain was excruciating, but it brought him a higher enlightenment.

With that in mind, I took that idea, personalized it, and turned it into a story. It's not really my area of expertise, thankfully, but it was in my periphery because Gen's band, Genitorturers, employed sadomasochistic elements as part of their stage show. It was also very interesting to me. There was a magazine out at the time called *Modern Primitives*, in which different people explored the path to Zen, as it were, and reportedly gained additional enlightenment in doing so.

On similar lines, I've studied a lot of Aleister Crowley's work. He had a very interesting way of thinking, no doubt chemically induced, and, as part of the salad bar of life, there are some lines of thinking in his work that interested me, as well as quite a bit that is left at the buffet. That's the case with everything: you attach yourself to any thinking that you find useful within the governance of your personal compass and your own likes and dislikes. You then formulate a recipe of thought that works best with you as an individual.

Perhaps this was an unusual subject for a death-metal song, but I didn't concern myself with that. I never held a finger up to the wind to check what was current or not. As you'll recall, there wasn't an awful lot going on in the direction that we were going in when we first started out. Although we had our various and sundry influences, it had not been amalgamated in the fashion that we were going at it, so we really weren't too concerned with what others were doing. We concerned ourselves only with what we were doing, so to that end I found inspiration in different places, connected emotionally with it, and made a story out of it.

• chapter five •

REBIRTH

"Therapy means finding that which is joyful. Here's how I realigned myself and dismissed my demons."

I didn't know what I wanted to do when I left Morbid Angel. I didn't know anything, other than that I needed to get myself together, so I just took some time off. I went up to the mountains in North Carolina for a while and decompressed, which wasn't uncommon for me. I did that from time to time to clear my mind. It's a very serene place, good for contemplation and internal dialogue.

I really felt that I needed a realignment. I felt as if I was out of touch with just about everything, other than this star persona that had gone so badly awry. I'd really let my ego get out of control, to the point where it was detrimental to myself and to everybody around me. So I knew I needed to get that in check. It didn't occur to me to leave for a period and then return; I simply said, 'That's it.' It was a snap decision.

Word traveled, and by the time we got home, Gunter and Trey had talked about it, and Gunter called me. I didn't have much to say. I was in decompression mode, and I wanted to be off the map. I spent what seemed like an eternity in internal dialogue.

I wasn't trying to end the band. I just wanted to extract myself. I remember Gunter saying that he didn't think it was a good idea, and my response was that it was the only idea.

After that, I felt that it was important to reconnect with humanity, to get grounded and down-to-earth, so I took a job as a taxicab driver in Tampa. It wasn't a highly paid job, but it wasn't about the money, it was about the interaction. I needed to get to the point where I could deal with things, and, honestly, I felt like it would be good therapy.

I'm not proud of the way I behaved toward the end of my time in Morbid Angel, but I would follow that up by saying that it was a necessary part of the process. I wouldn't be where I am today without having gone through that. Everything is part of a process and part of a portfolio—and, along with that, there are highs and lows. Sometimes you can find the pinnacle of being high right before you find out what happens when you literally fall from grace.

I had always liked myself, and now that I didn't it was time for a realignment. I found a more productive and more satisfying way to be that person. Later, I apologized to everyone—Trey, Gunter, Gen, my parents.

My solution was to take a long time off from music in order to follow a therapy regimen that I prescribed for myself. I had a lot of things to deal with, and I manage them to this day.

To begin with, I'm obsessive-compulsive. You may be familiar with an American TV series called *Monk*, which centers on a police detective who suffers from severe OCD, as I do. In my case, I start feeling really uncomfortable when things aren't as they should be, and I can't take my mind off of them. For instance, if things are not in the correct sequence, I'll fix them. I'll be at someone's house, and I'll be paralyzed until I rearrange the furniture. Someone could be calling my name at that time, and I don't even hear them because I'm fixated on something.

I couldn't watch *Monk* because it made me feel very uncomfortable. I knew exactly what this character was feeling, and I'd sit and wring my hands when it was on, or I'd have to get up and leave. Watch it if you want to know what I mean.

I also have a really bad attention-deficit disorder. I'm constantly between radio stations. I have little switches that I turn on or off, mentally, and I'm really bad with names, and I'll forget words.

I'll know what the word I want is, and I can see it, but I'll start compulsing and ask myself what it is. Or I'll meet someone who I know really well, but I get this block, and I'm between radio stations, so to speak. It's no fun.

The only thing I seem to remember really well is music. I never forget anything if it's catchy and it catches me; it's there for life. I'm not a casual listener or a casual watcher; my undivided attention goes to whatever it is. If I'm at a show and I'm there to see a band, and someone asks me for a photo, I can't do it. I literally have to go to shows with people who will stand around and keep others at bay. It's not because I'm stuck-up, believe me.

There were a couple of medications that seemed to help with these things quite a bit, but I didn't like the way that they made me feel, because they took my edge off, so I learned the difference between on and off and built my own switches, so that I wouldn't need to take the drugs.

This period of my life wasn't all bad, by any means. Gen and I were married on April 30, 1995, in a pagan wedding. It was a real spectacle, with a very diverse audience. Gunter was my best man. We wanted to avoid a Christian ceremony, so we asked an Icelandic scholar to lead the service. We banded arms and swore honor to the swords. The ceremony was something we crafted that was meaningful to us, and puzzling but entertaining for our guests.

Friends, family members, and our fellow musicians were there, as well as our grandmothers, who didn't understand a lot of it until we got to the music, which was all big-band tunes from the thirties and forties. They appreciated that. We really entertained ourselves, even down to placing people next to each other in a way that might cause a little tension. We both shared the same mischievous sense of humor in that way.

Gen and I were together for twenty years, and we had a lot of really good times, as well as sharing great music and wonderful travel. We were best friends, and although we eventually grew apart, we parted with mutual respect. She is someone who I will always look at as a good, talented, decent person.

Gen and I were never ready to have kids, and I hear from others that you have to not have a plan and just go for it. I wanted to be more deliberate than that, and as a result I'm childless. It's not like there's a lack of people in the world, but I'm told that I'd be a good father. Today, I would agree with that; some years ago, I would not have agreed.

As I mentioned earlier, for my first year away from the band, I worked as a taxicab driver. It was really interesting. I learned a lot, whether about myself or about others, from a much different vantage point than the one I'd had before. I learned about perception, and I learned about a lot of ways that I was very dismissive of certain types of people, and how stereotypes that I had in my mind manifested themselves in the real world.

Nobody believed that I was taking time out from the band to undergo my version of therapy. I remember when I first went down to the cab company, and they were like, 'Why are you doing this?' They were scratching their heads, because a lot of them knew who I was. I told them I needed to do it, and they were almost perplexed.

I was in a moment of self-humbling, so I was more incognito

than I would otherwise have been. I wasn't going in there as anyone other than a normal guy doing a normal thing. I didn't have a chip on my shoulder or a sign on my shirt. I was just another guy doing what those guys do.

After a few months, I had a few regular customers, one of whom was a young Arab guy from Qatar who was from a very wealthy family. He would ask me questions about American culture and why we think about things in this way or that way. It seemed like an interesting conversation, and we became comfortable in each other's company.

I made a lot of off-color comments about him and camels and other pejorative subjects, simply because I felt comfortable doing so. 'Having camels is actually a very prestigious thing,' he replied, 'almost like having racehorses is in the USA.' He seemed very entertained by my comments, and he was comfortable saying things to me that I was comfortable enough to say back.

I recall one day he called me up without anything in mind; there wasn't a particular errand or journey he needed to make. He wanted to go down to a motorcycle dealer, so I said, 'Sure, which one?' and he said, 'Somewhere I can find stuff that's fast.'

I took him to this one dealer in Tampa, and the way my Arab friend was dressed would not have led anyone to assume that he was a man of means. This place also sold watercraft—Jet Skis and so on—and I noticed that a couple of the salespeople looked at the two of us and evidently determined not to waste any time on us, because we obviously didn't have the means to buy these expensive vehicles.

I asked a few questions, and my friend told one of the sales staff, 'I want to get four of these, and a couple of these,' adding up to a purchase of six to eight vehicles, including watercraft. He wanted them to be shipped overseas. The guffaws coming from the sales guy indicated that he didn't want to waste any time on that conversation.

I found the sales manager and I said, 'Listen, don't let looks be deceiving; he's serious.'

My friend ended up making the purchase with the sales manager, not the salesman who had laughed at him. I looked over at the sales guy, and he was obviously thinking, *I didn't see that one coming.*

I thought to myself, *That idiot thinks the same way that I used to think.* My mind had been changed. You might see a man dressed in a tuxedo and that's all he has, or you could see a man dressed as if he slept in a cardboard box last night and he's rich. You don't know—we have tendencies to make decisions about things, and we feel like we're fully informed, but every now and then there's a curveball.

I have a million stories about the people I met in this way. When you drive people around, you're not just taking them from point A to point B—you're also somehow a life counselor or a psychiatrist along the way, depending on how far somebody wants to take it. A number of these experiences—and I could go on and on about things that I've thought, and opinions that I've formed, through both the briefest of interactions and the longest of rides—resembled a therapy session for people, a way to get a stranger's point of view or just to be able to talk to someone about something.

Each new thing that I learned on this job, and each meaningful conversation that I had, taught me a lot of empathy. I think that has always been a challenge for me—putting myself in someone else's shoes. It's not that I wasn't taught how to do it as a kid, I just don't think that it ever really manifested itself in me as something that was important.

It's not as if I deliberately ever walked away from these things. If I didn't feel something, I had to find a way to feel it. I would ask myself, *What can I do, and what situation can I put myself in, so that I can honestly internally assign importance to things?* It's not that I'm thinking, *Well, I don't care about people*—it's not that at all. It's more that if I don't feel something, I just don't feel something. I can fake it, because you can pretend you like something when you don't, if it's for someone else's benefit, and maybe that's worth doing at times.

In essence, I believe that in order to evolve, and extend the wisdom and motivation of that evolution to others, you've got to be there yourself first. This has been a path that I've been on forever, from childhood to growing up. Every little thing that I've ever done—from when I was a child, learning about and testing the system, and poking and prodding and provoking it—has all been the search for, *What is my Zen? Is it someone else's definition of Zen? Is it something I've been taught? Is it an amalgamation between the basics of culture, and taking the time to weigh out what the importance of those basics is for me? And, if so, how do I employ them in my day-to-day existence?*

All of my answers to these questions are only my 'today' answers, but I spent a lot of time looking for them, and I never stop searching, trust me. Of course, like anyone, I fall down. I allow situations to get the best of me, because I'm human. My goal and my desire is to continue to follow this path and to find a way to create new realizations for myself—but also extend that to other people, and to encourage others to do so.

Illuminating as my taxicab job was, music is not just a vocation for me; it's mandatory. I can't really turn it off. I don't have a choice in the matter, or at least it would be denying who I am if I didn't make music. It was obvious that there was a lot I could do to help Gen with Genitorturers, so I started working full-time with her after driving a taxicab for a year or so.

This was obviously different to my Morbid Angel role, because I wasn't standing out front with Gen's band. In fact, short of setting myself on fire, there was nothing I could do to get anyone's attention, because all eyes were fixed on her. This was a different movie in which I played a different character. It was Gen's show, and I was a good soldier.

I did different things with Genitorturers. I did a few backing vocals, and I snuck in a few backing tracks. Gunter was looking after them as well, and he really impressed on me that I should leave them to their own devices and not get too involved, as my instincts had been to do that, to a certain extent.

I really liked the songs. I'd always liked industrial music; in particular, I admire Trent Reznor of Nine Inch Nails, who is an amazing composer, with electronics as his instrument. Yes, Nine Inch Nails started as a pop sensation, but he intentionally drove it away from that, because he didn't want to be there, even though he was having hits. He has my absolute respect.

Genitorturers were an interesting band, and Gen really wanted to make it work, but at first she didn't think she could make money out of it, so I came along and tour-managed the band for a while. I used some of the skills I'd learned, such as making sure their merchandise was set up right and that the tour accounts were right—basically looking after some of the business side.

After some time, Gen got the attention of the IRS record label, and in particular Nick Turner of the band Lords Of The New Church, who was the A&R executive for IRS. The connection with IRS worked well because they also had a booking agency, Frontier Booking, which was run by the label's owner, Miles Copeland, brother of The Police's drummer, Stewart. Gen now had a record label and an agency, and so she went out on tour.

The Genitorturers show was themed in a scary, campy way, where they would pull people out of the audience and do to them whatever they could get away with. I got a kick out of it—it was very Alice Cooper–like and theatrical. There were times when she was between bass players, so I filled in at a couple of shows.

Genitorturers were a damn entertaining band, and I was certainly entertained by them. It was one of the most fun projects I've ever done. Gen was interested in the Marquis de Sade, who inspired the stage show, which had an evil carnival feel, and she was also very active in the fetish community.

I played on the *Sin City* album in 1998, and the *Machine Love* remix album in 2000. The band started calling me Evil D, and I got a kick out of it. It was kind of a joke, actually; I knew a lot of DJs, and one day I called up a friend of mine and I said, 'It's DJ Evil D!' in front of a group of people, who all started laughing. From that point on, they all started calling me that.

I was Genitorturers' fourth and sixth bass player, and I probably worked with a dozen or more musicians in the band. We always asked ourselves, *What direction are we going in this time?* I wrote a lot of songs sitting on the couch with an acoustic guitar; I'd have a simple idea and ask Gen what she thought, and she'd say if she liked it or not, and then I'd think about where her voice would work best.

Once, we were playing a show up in New York. Gene Simmons of KISS happened to be in the city and he heard that we were performing at this club, so he came down and got on the tour bus. I was in the back lounge with Gen, and a kid who was in the stage show came running in, saying, 'G-G-Gene's here!' so I went up there and said hello.

I asked, 'What are you doing, Gene?'

Gene said, 'I'm making money. What else would I be doing?'

He sat there talking to this kid in the show about fire breathing and how to do it safely. He was literally tutoring him about how to do it, which was really cool. Gen came out and said hello and told him that she would put him on the guest list for the show. He replied, 'No, I don't mind buying a ticket. I'm a big buyer of tickets.' Finally, Jonathan asked him if he could take a photo with him, and Gene asked him for five dollars! Just as a joke, of course. It was an endearing caricature.

I liked Gene. He's never off; he's always on. He's only ever been nice to me, but I've seen him reduce people to nothing in my presence. He came to see us play one night when we were in Hollywood, and some kid came up to him who I think was trying to put together a TV show, and he said, 'Gene, what would it take to get you on board?' He replied, 'Six figures. I'm no different than the whore standing on a street corner, I'm just more expensive.' That was his answer. This kid just cowered away.

Alice Cooper is another one of my favorites. He's relevant; he keeps his eye on things. He tried to engage me in conversation once involving religion, but I wasn't going to go there because I had too much respect for him, including his personal religious beliefs. It so happened that there is a big annual charity radio event in south Florida that Gen used to do; she was fairly regular guest on a rather raucous morning radio show. You could go to this outdoor picnic event and order food that was served to you by a well-known celebrity.

As it turned out, Alice was there at this weekend-long event and he wanted to meet Gen. She knew who he was but had never really been into his music, whereas I was, so I showed her some music and got her into it. They were talking and visiting amicably and they got along well, and she said, 'You know, my husband's a really big fan of yours, and he'd love it if you signed something for him.'

Alice said, 'Oh, yeah, that's the Morbid Angel guy, right? I'll sign something for him, but tell him to turn his cross the right side up.'

Fast forward a couple of years, and Alice was playing in New Orleans, so Gen and I took a road trip from Tampa to see him. We met with him backstage afterward, and I was being on my best, sunny behavior, because this guy was my hero when I was a kid. I was really into the dark imagery, the storytelling—it was excellent.

So I was there with all my CDs, asking him to sign them, and while he was doing that, he starts this conversation. 'So, what is it about Tampa and all this satanic death metal? If they want to kill Christians, they can start with me—I'm right here!'

I didn't take the bait. I just said, 'Oh, I think it's just a lot of show,' and threw it to one side.

Now, if it had been anybody else, I would have engaged in a spirited discussion, but I had too much respect for him to go there. It's fine. You think what you think, and I'll think what I think. I know what Alice's beliefs are—and I'm good with that.

I also had a small professional-wrestling promotion in Tampa, which I ran with two partners. It wasn't a huge organization, but we made it look as huge as we could on a pauper's budget. It was a success, and I'll tell you why.

A lot of professional wrestlers live in the Tampa area, and there are a lot of wrestling schools there, some of which are really good. If a wrestler had been trained at one of two particular schools, I had no hesitation in booking a match and putting them in the ring. I knew that they would not have gotten released from one of these two places without knowing their shit.

A lot of these guys were semipro—in other words, they had day jobs—so I worked with these people on their shtick, or their persona. That's something that many of them had no clue about, although they knew their ring techniques. I would look at their strong and weak points, and we'd figure out a way that we could create a persona that put them over to the audiences. If you're a wrestler, I don't care if they're cheering you, booing you, or laughing at you—any one of those is great, because then people are involved. If you go into the ring and the members of the audience turn their backs and go and get a drink from the bar, that's what you don't want.

I worked with a lot of these guys. At first, they didn't trust me, because I'm not a wrestler, although one of my partners was. He sat them all down and said, 'Listen, if David tells you something, you ought to listen to it, because when it comes to performing and understanding that side of things, he knows what he's talking about.'

They warmed up eventually, but it took me a while to earn their trust. Part of the schooling of these guys—at least in the old days—was, *You don't trust someone who's not one of us.* Their mindset is very similar to that of the carnies.

We had some really neat angles that we created. There were a couple of Mexican guys who I never booked, but they had so much heart. They heard that we ran a show once a month, so they would show up in the hopes that they would have a chance to work. They weren't particularly talented, and they were a little sloppy in the way that they worked, but the bigger problem was that their image was lacking, so people didn't really care about them.

I came up with an angle and shared it with my partner first. He laughed, so I told them, 'Here's what we're gonna do. The two of you don't speak English anymore. One of you speaks English, but he's the mouthy one, and he has to translate what the other one says from Spanish into English.'

We would create these multipart slapstick comedy routines where they went up as a tag team against these two big biker guys from north Florida. They called themselves the Long Riders, and they were mean-spirited redneck guys who weren't really quick in the ring, but they were ominous. It was like a play—everybody knows their spot and rolls with it.

The Long Riders came in and yelled, 'We're gonna send your asses back to Mexico where you belong!' and the Mexicans would look at each other and ask, 'What did he say?' in Spanish, and then ask the referee to explain. They would go back and forth with explanations, and then start laughing—which would endear the crowd to them.

All this made two unremarkable wrestlers into people that everybody loved. I saw the reactions of the audiences: they laughed hysterically and really liked the guys. They'd be cheering for them. Before that, audiences were like, *Whatever*—which is the worst reaction you can have.

Another wrestler was a tall, lanky guy who came in one night, and he had stuck a sock in his trousers so it looked like he was hung like a racehorse. He did it as a joke, because he had on some new wrestling tights, and all the other guys were making fun of him. I walked in, saw this, and immediately said, 'You're doing that in the ring. No arguments!' I knew it would be funny when the referee checked each wrestler for foreign objects at the start of the match.

It worked, too; the house came down with laughter, especially as we changed his ring name to Big Dick and then added his surname. It was all this kind of slapstick humor, which people thought was a lot of fun. We ran it once a month and divided up the money that we made among the wrestlers. We also videotaped all the matches, with decent commentary and instant replays and little vignettes, and we gave those videos to the guys, who used them to land bigger jobs.

That's how I count it as a success, not because it made much money for me personally, but because it helped people to refine their game and move upward in their careers. I did it for a couple of years—it was a really fun time.

I also started working with Dean Guitars, doing their trade shows and giving them a little bit of assistance with their artist relations, because I knew a lot of people and they were looking to increase their roster. I helped to pull in my friends Dimebag Darrell, Karl Sanders, and Michael Angelo Batio, among others, to Dean.

I remember enjoying Michael's guitar solos with his band Nitro back in the eighties; their videos were so over-the-top it was ridiculous, and in hindsight I don't know how seriously it was taken by anyone, but those solos were incredible. I played some for Trey and he said, 'Man, that guy is really going for it.' Michael played so cleanly and precisely. I watched his *Star Licks* video, and even as a bass player I learned a lot from him. Nobody played like that, even at a time when there were a lot of shredding guitar players who were all trying to play faster than each other—not unlike death-metal drummers.

Michael gets an *A* for precision, with no delay or reverb to hide anything that wasn't on point. You have to have respect for people who have spent the years that it takes to perfect that technique when all their friends were out drinking and chasing girls.

Throughout this time, I don't think I missed being in Morbid Angel. I was pretty happy, having overcome a lot of things and put them behind me. Gen really helped me with a lot of that by being very encouraging and supportive. We were both type-A personalities, and I had to learn not to walk in and take over the conversation; again, it was about learning empathy and measuring things, which I previously had no ability to do. This was all part of my evolution.

I became a better person because I got happy. I learned to redirect the anger that I felt. I looked at things differently, too. I still have an ego—you have to, otherwise you'd be scared to go out and get in the car—but it's a healthy ego.

Thinking back to how uneventful the turn of the millennium was, it seems funny to think that it was ever a cause for concern, but at the end of 1999, I was worried. I had a very good friend who owned a large server company in the Tampa area, and he was out purchasing generators and food and weapons.

I said, 'What's going on?'

He said, 'There's going to be a serious problem.'

As he was obviously closer to the technological side than I was, I was concerned, too, but of course I already had a generator and weapons, as I always have. I mention that here because it's relevant to my earlier point about the necessity of survival skills. There's nothing like having an umbrella before it rains, after all.

The real seismic shock of this period came, of course, on September 11, 2001. I remember my phone ringing at some ridiculous time in the morning, when I was at home. I recognized the number and picked up, knowing that it must be important if someone was calling at this time of day.

The friend who had called me said, 'Oh my God. A plane just crashed into the World Trade Center.'

I said, 'What?' and turned on the news. While I was watching the news, the second plane went in. I knew right then that something was really fucked.

My mind was immediately scrambling: *All right, I need to make sure we get through this*. I checked that we had plenty of nonperishable food, because it was very clearly a serious attack. One plane might be an accident—albeit a freak accident—but two was obviously deliberate. The news then said that all flights were grounded, and given that the United States is a rather large country, what did that mean? If something that big could get through this massive protection network that we have, how could this be?

It was really a shock to all Americans. It was not knowing what had happened that was so bad, because all we could do is guess. Later that day, a few politicians went on TV and made comments, and of course I'm immediately suspicious of anything that a politician says. I'm doubly suspicious when there's a cause-and-effect reaction, and when a government—in this case my government—puts a spin on something in a way that allocates blame, especially as I know as a student of history that history repeats itself.

I think that day changed the world. It has had very far-reaching consequences. There are natural disasters that claim greater loss of life, of course—earthquakes, tsunamis, hurricanes—and these events are not wanted, but they're expected. Killings that are deliberate are a whole other realm.

As you know by now, I'm not a huge fan of authority per se. I do think we need a general set of rules to live by, in order to keep society between the ditches, but I'm not a big fan of religion, especially the way it has historically been used as a manipulator and has inspired people into negative activities of which we've all seen evidence. For thousands of years, there have been different brands of religious atrocities from all sides, with the possible exception of the Buddhists.

I know that there were many people who were warned not to show up to work on the day that the planes hit the World Trade Center. I also know that there was communication between people, alerting them that something was going to happen. I think that a lot more people knew that something was up than we've been led to believe.

I'm sad to say that at this point I believe that there are some ulterior motives, and that we have not been told the entire truth about the story. I know that the reaction from what happened resulted in a further reach by our government into the lives of the average American citizen, and I know that the military-industrial complex suddenly got a very large order—one that they were happy to take.

When I think back to history, I'm reminded of the sinking of the British ship the RMS *Lusitania* in the northern Atlantic in 1915. It was known that the area was controlled by German U-Boats, and it enabled the USA to enter World War I two years later. I can't help but ask myself what the difference is between the *Lusitania* and the World Trade Center attacks. I don't think it's unreasonable to draw that comparison.

"I've talked about some abstract themes in this chapter, but they boil down to this: if a day goes by where I'm unable to take something into consideration in a way that I haven't done before, or that I don't experience something that adds to my frame of reference, I feel that I've cheated myself. I really do believe that. The further I go, the further I feel I have to go. The journey is ongoing. The journey will only end when they close the casket lid."

GOD OF EMPTINESS

FROM *COVENANT*, 1993

Lies, and you'll fill their souls
With all impressions of this world,
And all the glory you'll receive?
So what makes you supreme?
Lies, and your crown is falling.
I offer fantasy, and you
Create the blind with envy

Let the children come to me
Their mother loves me, so shall they
Woman, bleeding, ate my gifts
Man was close behind
Just like a snake I'm slithering
Through my world divine
And like the cat I'm stalking
I'll take your soul and you'll be like me
In emptiness, free

Just bow to me faithfully
Bow to me splendidly

I was visiting my parents when I wrote this song, and I used to have this little microcassette recorder by the side of the bed. I did this because I'd often come up with songs just as I was drifting into sleep, and I'd tell myself, *That's so good, there's no way I'll forget it,* and then I'd wake up the next morning and think, *What the hell was that?* I used to force myself to wake up and get these ideas onto tape, lest they be gone forever. Gifts come to us in different ways and at different times, and it's up to us to harvest them.

Having said that, I woke up and narrated the whole 'Let the children come to me / Their mother loves me, so will they' part, which has a lot of Biblical references.

It just so happened that upon my return, some months later, the musical foundation for that very song existed, and it worked perfectly. It's a very dreamy song, and the first time we'd ever done something like that. We knew it was a good song, so we left it to be the last song on the record.

We got a lot of flak for 'God Of Emptiness,' though, because it was out of left field. As time went on, I noticed that different kinds of people were coming to the shows because of it. They'd stand at the back for most of the set and then, when it came to 'God Of Emptiness,' they'd come and stand at the front. The demographic was mostly ghoulish goth chicks who came for that one song, which was interesting, because when we played it, a lot of folks were like, *Hmm, I don't know about this.* It was very different, and the slow fade at its end leaves you hanging in a bleak emptiness.

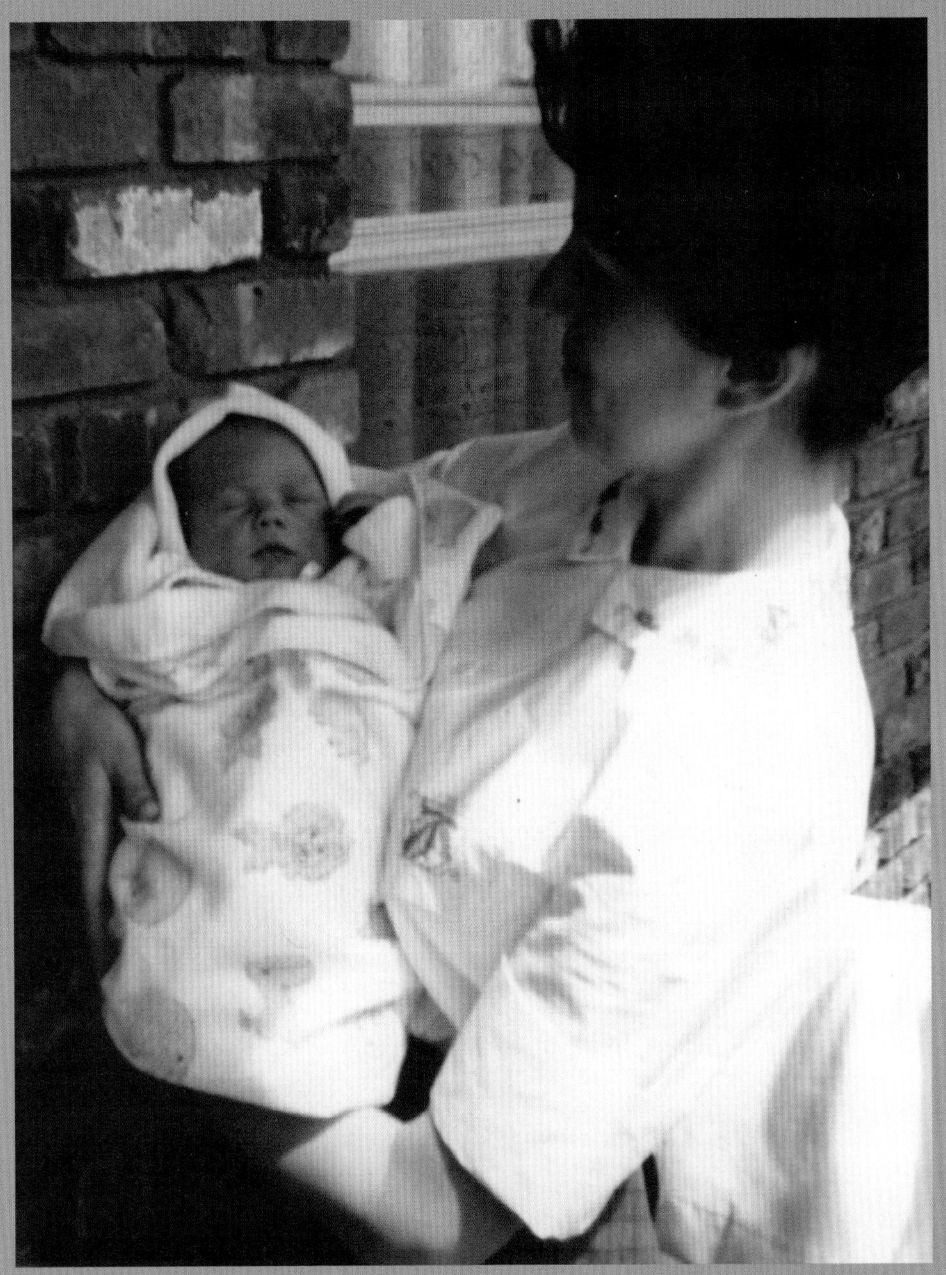

ABOVE Five days old, with ten fingers and ten toes—all good so far.

LEFT Eight months in the womb—only one more to go!

ABOVE One year old and still happy.

ABOVE Six years old with my youngest brother. *Take a break, Mom. I've got this.*

RIGHT Two-and-a-half years old with my mother and middle brother.

ABOVE First day of school, age six. *Do I have to go?*

LEFT Seven years old with my first pet, Charlie the chameleon.

BELOW Saturday in the park.

ABOVE Age twelve, showing my cousin some chords.

BELOW Fourteen years old, jamming with Cousin Jim.

TOP Miss my buddy Roman. Been rescuing dogs ever since.

ABOVE Two grannies and me—lucky to have them in my life.

RIGHT I love the sound of old pump organs.

ABOVE The Morbid tour bus stops off in North Carolina during the US tour of 1988. *Left to right*: Trey Azagthoth, Richard Brunelle, David Vincent, Pete Sandoval.

RIGHT Rehearsing in late '88, around the time *Altars Of Madness* was recorded.

ABOVE Tuning up backstage in Jackson at the Michigan Deathfest, August 1990.

ABOVE The American Madness tour hits Jackson, Michigan, summer 1990.

ABOVE Rocking the Chance in Poughkeepsie, New York, as the American Madness tour rolls into 1991.

LEFT Backstage in Bayshore, Long Island, August 1990. *Left to right*: David Vincent, Pete Sandoval, Richard Brunelle, Trey Azagthoth.

ABOVE Preparing to take the stage at the Milwaukee Deathfest, August 1994. *Left to right*: Pete Sandoval, Erik Rutan, Trey Azagthoth, David Vincent.

RIGHT Back on the road with Morbid Angel at the With Full Force Festival in Löbnitz, Germany, July 2008.

ABOVE Headlining the Marquee II stage at Graspop Metal Meeting in Dessel, Belgium, June 2008.

LEFT Back on the European festival circuit for Wacken Open Air in Wacken, Germany, August 2011.

RIGHT Irving Plaza, New York City, November 2013.

BELOW On the US leg of the *Illud Divinum Insanus* tour at City National Grove, Anaheim, California, October 2012.

ABOVE Stalking the stage at Slim's, San Francisco, November 2013.

ABOVE Shooting the video for 'Drinkin' With The Devil' at J. Lorraine Ghost Town in Manor, Texas, February 2016.

LEFT The live debut of my outlaw country band at the White Horse Saloon in Austin, Texas, April 2016.

OPPOSITE TOP LEFT Onstage with I Am Morbid at the Whisky A Go-Go, Hollywood, California, January 2019.

OPPOSITE TOP RIGHT With Vltimas at the Alcatraz Festival in Kortrijk, Belgium, August 2019.

OPPOSITE BOTTOM Vltimas in Woburn, England, May 2017. *Left to right*: Rune Eriksen, David Vincent, Flo Mounier.

ABOVE With Morbid Angel at the Fonda Theater in Los Angeles, November 2013, during the US leg of the tour celebrating the twentieth anniversary of *Covenant*.

RIGHT At the O2 Islington Academy in London, England, with *Rosetta* Mission Project Scientist Dr. Matt Taylor of the European Space Agency, December 2014.

DOMINATE

FROM *DOMINATION*, 1995

Weak aside, no place for those our struggle
Leaves behind
Our Lord won't tolerate those whom through
Attrition fall
We must dominate!

With iron through our veins and a will made so elite
Hunting for our daily bread and the sinister close in sight
Hunger always drives the beast and the women fall prey.

Leading all the wonders to certain fate
Another victim reviled
I'm staring at you through the eyes of the wolf
Tell me who is going to save you now!

Animal senses ever alert
Praise be to the father-war
As a servant I am serving myself and I bathe in anticipation
Unless you taste it you could never know
All the power our Lord bestows
With a bow and a kiss profane
Be a victor or be a victim

This album started with pure attack, and I felt as though 'Dominate' drove the point home well. Obviously, songs such as 'Caesar's Palace' and 'Inquisition' aren't as heavy or as fast as others, but they add to the story. There's comedy and tragedy in everything, and opening with 'Dominate' was just a ripper.

It was funny: we were signed to Warner Bros at the time, and they had all these advisors who would tell their bands to do this and this. They had nothing to say to us, though. We were probably a lot different from any of the other artists that they had—so we just did what we did, and the album came together as organically as possible. Fortunately for me, I was working with tremendous musicians who were extremely creative, and we made a good team.

WHERE THE SLIME LIVE

FROM *DOMINATION*, 1995

Where the slime live
(They are the lowest forms of life)
Where the slime breed
(They make a new one too corrupted)
When the wind blows
(The winds of truth are blowing now)
And the cradle falls down

Their poison fingers that wrote the poison lines
Their poison lingers
What a tragedy when their fingers are removed

Where the slime live

Their burning dogma
Introducing to our mind lies
They plot for the total control of the morals
And what a tragedy when the god-heads are removed.

They crawl, they breed, they hide but we see
They burn
I see the smoke of the funerals rising
God lives in their heads now laid to rest

What a sight
As their kingdom comes tumbling down
We burn … the ones with contrite souls be gone!

Long gone are the filthy liars
Long gone are their filthy lies
I know they'll come again some day
Where the slime live and how the slime gets washed away

The riff in this song grabbed me as soon as I heard it. The way Trey described it, even before I heard it, made me see exactly what I wanted to do. The lyrics came together really quickly, because I had such a vision, and I knew it was going to be a lot of fun. It's still one of my favorite songs to perform.

The way the riff works, it reminded me of the swamps in Yellowstone National Park, where there are bubbling mudflats that never stop. That's what I heard, so I wanted the whole vocal approach to be done in a repulsive but funny way.

The song in general is about the system being judgmental about anything that it doesn't like: the same people who would call *me* slime, I'm turning it around on them to face the mirror. I've had all manner of experiences of being profiled since I was a kid, just for looking like a metal guy and having my particular beliefs, and for some of the activities that I've chosen to be involved with over the years.

Still, it's metaphorical: you could equate the word slime to an undesirable person. That's what I was always referred to as, so I'm just turning the song back around, and calling them that. The line about fingers being removed was a funny dig at certain journalists who I'd had some words with. It was just really mocking, and thematically it really worked with the general unpleasantness of the vibe.

There are always naysayers. At the end of the day, I'm a man with an opinion, and any journalist is just another person who also has an opinion. Opinions are like assholes, everybody has one. Perhaps things are different these days: after all, how important are magazines now, and how important is music? The reverence that was once placed on both sides has been diminished. Yes, a writer might say a certain thing, but then again, thanks to social media, everyone's a writer these days.

· chapter six ·

HEAVEN AND HELL

"Governments. Religion. God. Do we really need any of them? Cars and bikes are more fun, as is traveling the world, as I realized more and more during my eight-year break from Morbid Angel."

As my therapy progressed and I learned about empathy, my thoughts crystalized on many subjects—and, as a man who is interested in the human condition and how it manifests itself, I came to a deeper appreciation of how Western society works … and doesn't work.

As you'll have grasped by now, I don't like government intrusion in anything. In America, they do a very poor job with education, they do a poor job with housing, they do a poor job with veterans' affairs. Everything they do, they do a very poor job of it.

When Barack Obama became president in 2009, he had the opportunity to be the great mender, in a lot of senses, but I thought his healthcare plans were terrible. Historically speaking, what evidence is there to make me believe that the government is somehow going to do a good job—after doing such a terrible job at everything else—with healthcare, one of the largest industries of all? I'm a very self-reliant person; I don't want to ask my government for help, and I don't want them asking things of me. I'm much more charitable when someone's not picking my pocket.

The only thing our government is good at—because they can't manipulate it, although they've done a good job of trying to do so—is our military, which is second to none. That involves a lot of private-sector folks, too, but the training that these heroes go through to be the most badass forces in the world is incredible. I'm friends with a lot of those people.

The other major establishment in America is the church. Now, clearly the religious establishment was a huge part of Morbid Angel's lyrical inspiration, especially in the early days, because our songs were so strongly rebellious against religion, but there is a deeper basis to it than mere rebellion.

Personally, I regard myself as somewhere between a Satanist and a pagan—there's an amalgamation there. I'm not generally a joiner, but I've been a quote-unquote card-carrying member of the Church of Satan for some time. I'd always been interested in it, so I joined in the late eighties. There is no tangible benefit to joining, but I believe that the original *Satanic Bible* that the founder, Dr. Anton LaVey, wrote in 1969 is a really good introduction to rebellious thought.

There are a lot of interpretations of Satanism. Essentially it's a selfish approach, and I don't mean that in a negative sense. When you come to the realization that I have, and that I believe—that the man in the mirror is ultimately the man in charge, and your belief system is not something that is answering to something outside of yourself—it's a position of strength.

Some of the myths of religious belief were created over the centuries to control people; obviously, we can look back at the socioeconomic and historical ramifications of how and why things were done for that reason. My belief is really the antithesis of Christianity, which states that there is a god—a force that we are answerable to. I would argue that we're only answerable to ourselves. In that sense, Satanism is selfish, because you're identifying the self as the being. Every person is an island, and when you strengthen that and identify that and become at one with that, there are an awful lot of ways to do things from a position of strength.

The person in the mirror is the life-giver, the source of knowledge, and it's up to me and the guy in the mirror in our conversations to make decisions that will go however they're going to go, whatever the ramifications of those things are. Independent thought is rebellious against the institutional thinking that comes from an overreaching government or a paternalistic religion. Buddhists are the exception to this; some of their practice seems like it's closer to this, although there's still a manner of groupthink involved.

The Christian church was much more powerful in the eighties than it is now. In the early days, say between 1987 and '89, there was quite a lot of Christian protesting at Morbid Angel shows. We were really in-your-face about it, and we were provocative, and some of these groups responded in kind. They thought we were making the devil's music, and they didn't want it, because it was poisoning the kids' minds, and so on. I knew better, but the media sensationalized it, television reporters showed up, and it became a phenomenon. At the end of the day, it was really good for business.

Nowadays, my attitude toward those people is, *Okay, don't buy a ticket*, but back then I was much more combative. Anything we did was against all odds; against all reasonable probabilities. We were in the face of people saying, *No, no, no, no!* and we still overcame them. We derived a sense of power from keeping our core unit strong and refusing to accept that which we didn't want to hear. That was our success.

I don't fault the protesters for standing up for their own beliefs. I don't think that religion is a powerful enough force to crush artistry, though. In any case, the whole world has become considerably more secular since then. Any of the things that were done in the past in the name of Christ—such as the Crusades—or the Catholic Church, nowadays we can see with 20/20 vision that a lot of it had very little to do with belief and much more to do with the harnessing of power and wealth.

Branches of Islam convince their followers that martyrdom for their cause is a good thing, which I find loathsome, and I also have no respect for religions that have no respect for women. That should be enough to make any sane individual, no matter how liberal they may be, question whether these things are necessary. How anyone can accept the degradation and even mutilation of women is beyond me; it says a lot about the insecurities of men who subscribe to those beliefs. There needs to be evolution. The earth is female, and these things should be celebrated, not repressed.

I never sought a role within the Church of Satan, although I was approached a lot, especially after Dr. LaVey's death in 1997. Being on tour was funny from that point of view. A fellow would come on the tour bus, self-styled, with that look, and say, 'So, we're thinking of recruiting more people to the church,' and that's where it would stop, because I would say, 'I don't want to recruit people. They need to have the strength to find it on their own. Otherwise, we don't want them.' But they never understood that; they would look at me like I was speaking a different language.

As for being a pagan, I believe I'm part of something, but not part of something other than the process. All around us, we're part of an organic entity, no different from any other species that shares this planet. We're born, we live, we die. There are people who contribute along the way, and there are those who are unremarkable, and I would hope that I am among the former category.

I'm friends with people with all sorts of beliefs, and none of it is uncomfortable for me. If it's uncomfortable for someone else, I choose not to discuss it with them. Why would you want to convince somebody to come your way? They'll find it on their own, which is necessary if you want to build an elite rather than just build numbers. Nothing is as important if you simply give it to a person as it is if they work for it, because then they're invested in it.

My other spiritual inspirations are many and diverse. H.P. Lovecraft was an inspiration for some of my occult lyrics, although his work wasn't occult per se: it was based on real beliefs and their fantastical interpretations. I've also studied quite a bit of the Kabbalah of Jewish mysticism, and of course Aleister Crowley was an interesting thinker, too. My favorite work of his is *The Book Of Lies* from 1912, because it is the most direct, and it reveals a lot about his thought processes. He was a very deep thinker.

Then there is the Marquis de Sade, who was an amazingly philosophical fellow, although that is only detectable if you're able to read past the complete degeneracy of some of the perverse things that he wrote. There are some very strong, independent words of wisdom in his work. When someone is shocked beyond belief, they pay attention; he wrote some of these things as attention-getters, and once he got your attention you quickly realized that he was very pro independent thought. He was also very rebellious against the Christian church and its doctrines.

I have been a student of the Left-Hand Path for as long as I can remember, and I would submit that the Marquis was an absolute Satanist, although he didn't define himself as such. He was very critical of church teachings, and a number of the points that he made were ultimately echoed in later teachings such as those of Dr. LaVey.

As I see it, there's a theme in the work of a long line of these thinkers, from Plato onward, and it is based on the notion of thinking outside the box. In order to successfully do so, and to challenge yourself, you really have to dismiss the accepted paradigms of the day. You have to allow yourself to feel comfortable drifting into areas that were considered heretical thought at different times, and which are not part of the mainstream.

All of these thinkers, from the early pioneers all the way through to Friedrich Nietzsche and modern-day philosophers like Tony Robbins, have written about finding ways to get in touch with the person in the mirror. It's not a question of finding comfort or solace in standard beliefs; it can be secular, it can be religious, but it's essential to know that awareness starts with your own personal strength and confidence. Once you accept that as a premise, you're able to look at things objectively, with an ability to command your mind without worrying what other people are thinking.

Once you reach that point, everything starts working for you. You can become your own prophet, and you can design answers that work for you, because you're not bound by concerns with that which is or has been. As a strong individual, you're also a strong link in the chain of the process of which we are all a part.

People have a different take on the nature of deep thought: for me, it's all about strength through open-mindedness. Any form of maverick thought has historically been disquieting to the masses, but it leads our species to amazing advances. The renegades—the true artistes of thought and work—were all heretics. Heresy is the one thing that has historically led to growth and evolution. It is the constant factor in all overachievement and greatness.

Christian religious thought does not appeal to me because it assigns the ultimate godhead to someone other than the individual.

That said, the basic teachings of the Christian faith, from a societal standpoint, do offer some broadly sound ideas. Treat others as you would like to be treated. Don't steal. Don't lie. These are basic, honorable understandings which are required, because we have societies which need to function, so they're fundamental. I agree with those things entirely, but I don't accept the premise that there is some punishment for malice outside of that which you would find here on Earth.

As a scare tactic, that idea worked for years, and it probably kept some people going who needed the idea of the supernatural. As Christianity spread through northern Europe, and its proponents proselytized with a list of commandments that people had to obey, the more aware of those who listened would recognize these commandments as sensible things that already existed within their regional 'pagan' beliefs.

Given that, what was the point of replacing one religion with another? Ultimately, it was a political game involving monarchies, trade, and power: what better way to unite everybody than to have everyone believe the same thing and scare them into thinking that other beliefs would harm them? Horrible crimes were committed in the name of ramming Christianity down people's throats—crimes that would be excommunicable under their very own Christian doctrine.

Again, an individual Christian who finds comfort and solace in their belief, perhaps because it creates peace for them and is a tradition in their family, should not be prevented from doing so. I don't want to attack someone for their beliefs, because I don't like being attacked for mine. There's a lot of commonality with the way that I practice my life and the practice of a good Christian. We simply have much different motivations.

Organized religion does, in any case, take a back seat to corporate puppeteering in most people's lives these days. Governments facilitate the whims of the profiteers who pay for politicians to be elected. You may or may not choose to buy into the idea that we have a representative government. On a local level, you can see tangible things being done in your community, and you can actively improve day-to-day life within that community—but once you get to a national and international level, there are absolutely scandalous and undeniably devious things that are lobbied for and enacted that are nowhere near being in the best interests of the citizenry. I loathe that. Just as I dislike organized religion, I despise crony politics and the way that it is realized. This is true evil.

The Catholic Church was a regular part of my childhood. I liked the music, and I sang in the choir for that reason—I just don't agree with the lyrics. I didn't believe a word that I was singing. I like the music to this day, especially the classically inspired hymns. It evolved from a good intent, but it starts with the belief that we're all bad, and I just find that demoralizing.

I look at the idea of a Christ figure in the same way that I look at a government. It's something that is there for comfort, but also as a threat of something bad that will happen to you if you don't follow the rules. If something makes sense, and there's a moral code that you live your life by, then for me there doesn't need to be a threat of punishment, whether it's being arrested or going to hell.

I see very little difference in any of these things. Either people are good with themselves or they're not, and if they're not, hopefully they find a way to become good with themselves, because if you're good with yourself it's easier to find a way to be good with others—as I've found out myself.

I believe in an afterlife, but not in the way that it is usually portrayed. It's really simple. There is immortality in the form of living on in the hearts and minds of others—in the form of genetic lineage in your offspring. Your works also exist after you, if you leave an indelible mark. These are tangible things that cannot be denied, even though people add to them with their belief system. This is an absolute truth of immortality that can't be dismissed. Everything else beyond that involves creative thinking or faith.

We're no different from any other living or organic thing on this planet. Just because we have a higher level of cognizance than a mouse, it doesn't mean that we're better. The tangible way that we can evidence this, with no faith involved, is that we come from our ancestors, and our offspring follow, and this will continue until this world destroys itself, which may well happen.

My parents always taught me to question. What would be the most logical outcome in a given situation? This applied in the early days of Morbid Angel, when we had to deal with aggressive, racist elements in our audience. On one early tour, we were playing on the same bill as Entombed, the Swedish death-metal band. Entombed had a black guitar player who was a really good fellow. There was a group of skinheads in the audience who were being racially abusive and spitting at him. I know there are a lot of different people in the world with different beliefs, but this was totally inappropriate.

I put my arm around him onstage and said, 'This guy's my

friend.' The skinheads left, or were forced to leave. Good. We ended up having a great show and a great tour.

Conversely, we played a show where a group of skinheads were ejected before we played—not because they had caused any trouble, but simply because the promoter and security staff didn't want them there—and I refused to play unless they were allowed back in. It's not really about what somebody believes, as I see it; it's about how they behave. If they act inappropriately, they should be taken to task; if they're acting appropriately, but they're being profiled, that's just as wrong.

I've always tried to view *Star Trek*'s Mr. Spock as a role model and ask myself what is logical here. Does something need to be addressed? If so, let's address it. Rules and expectations should be the same for everyone, no matter what group they belong to, and no matter what their ideology is.

That logical approach has worked well for me, especially because, as I said, I was taught as a kid to question the world, and not to accept things at face value. Find wisdom in the lessons of history: what has happened before often has relevance to what lies ahead. Being positive is also beneficial. I take things that used to be obstacles and I turn them into advantages. If that's the higher meaning of this book then it's a noble one.

Government and churches aside, the basic way that society is set up in the West doesn't necessarily suit me. I lived in the city of Tampa for many years, and in some ways it was convenient. I could walk home from the entertainment district if I knew I was going out on a power-partying session, or pay very little for a cab each way.

At the same time, I like differences, and there is no greater difference between shaking hands with hundreds of people per day and always being in the mix—which I enjoy—and getting out into nature. When I get home from a tour, I need some decompression time, so I go to the mountains for a month or whatever. All the pent-up stuff comes out. Meditation and relaxation is really important for me, and what better place to do it than in nature amid beautiful landscapes, where you can get back in touch with being a part of the biology of the planet?

Travel is also a panacea for the soul, although I prefer a tour bus to flying. I'm rather claustrophobic, to the point where I begin to feel anxious and ill if I'm in a mall and bumping into people: I feel as if I can't breathe and I need to get out of there. I have antianxiety medication that I take, but I don't like doing it except for the worst of circumstances, such as flying.

Life on the road is fun—from my perspective, at least—because I always view it as an adventure. I can go to a new place and meet new people and eat new food and explore differences. We have a huge planet.

I remember when I was at the Hellfest in Clisson, France, and I got in a taxi and told the driver just to drive in a certain direction. After a while, we came to a beautiful country house with a great restaurant. I had a wonderful experience there, and it's only in my memory: it's not about taking pictures to show people afterward.

I enjoy traveling, and I enjoy the differences between countries and cultures. For me, it's not about whether it's better somewhere else or not; it's about enjoying the differences between countries and languages, and how music can connect all these things, even though they're different.

For example, I really like South America a lot, and I always have. There's a passion there that is a cultural thing. Not all those countries are the same, either, but there's a general warmth and appreciation, which I return to the people because I get it. Of course, Europe is great, too; Europe's been great for me for many years. And although it's becoming more amalgamated now, there are still a large number of countries and languages there.

Touring was a very different business back then. Before they invented cellphones, I'd be trying to make calls home, and figuring out what the local currency was and where I could go to find a pocketful of change to feed the payphones. It was so damn expensive—I could barely put the money in fast enough to keep the call connected. Sure, it's convenient to have the euro these days, but I miss the deutschmarks and the guilders and the francs; there was something about those currencies that spoke to each of these places as its own entity. I liked that because, as I said, I like differences.

I try to conduct myself in a polite and respectful way when I'm in different countries. If English is not someone's first language and that person chooses to speak to me in English, I respect that. I love Japan, and English is not real common there. You can speak English just about anywhere in Europe and someone will understand you, but that's not the case in Japan, so it's good to have someone with you who can help with translation.

I love Australia, too. When I first went there in the nineties, it reminded me of America back in the seventies. Folks were really friendly, and the general way that people roll down there made me feel as though I was in America. I'm really into nature, so when I'm Down Under I always take the opportunity to go and visit the nature reserves. As it was so isolated, evolution dealt Australia some interesting cards when it comes to the plants and animals that don't exist anywhere else. You can see them in a zoo, but I'd much rather see an animal in its own environment than in a cage. The only drag about Australia is that it's so damn far away, and the flight is just miserable.

On that note, I don't think anybody likes flying. If it's longer than a couple of hours, I really need to spend the extra money and fly business class so I don't feel jammed in. I literally start feeling like I'm having a panic attack and can't breathe. On the bus, though, I had my spot: I would find my own space and sleep a lot, which you need to do on the road anyway. I do the show, have a few cocktails, go to sleep, wake up the next day, get up and move around, and then sleep again, following the two-sleep system that I mentioned earlier.

Maybe travel suits me because I've always liked vehicles, and specifically fast cars. This goes back to when I was a kid. Back then there were three or four of us who were into hot rods, to the point where we would actually build our own cars on the weekends. We'd go to junkyards and pull parts off cars. We each had a vehicle, and we'd soup them up and do car-related things. All the money we had from our after-school jobs would go into the cars.

My father felt that my brothers and I should have transportation, so he bought us a 1972 VW Beetle. He got it when I was fifteen, when I could get a learner's permit. Right after that I bought a 1968 Pontiac GTO with the money I earned from summer jobs—a bit of lifeguarding at a pool, a little bit of golf caddying, some mowing of lawns—whatever it took until I got my first official job at a warehouse after school for a textile-machine parts warehouse. North Carolina was a big textiles state with a lot of mills. They'd run the mills 24/7, so they'd break, and I'd have the parts to fix them.

At fifteen, I couldn't register or drive the Pontiac yet, but on the day I got it, my father was out of town. Most of my friends were older than I was, and when he came home, he couldn't pull into our driveway because all these cars were parked there, and we were all listening to music and making noise. My car was in the garage, where I was installing some header pipes. He was annoyed that he couldn't park in his own driveway and had to park down the street.

I remember being called for dinner and saying that I was busy, which annoyed my dad more. He became even more annoyed when I fired up the car while the exhaust still had open headers. It was so loud that the resonance made his glass of wine vibrate off the table and into his lap. He was already a little pissed off about getting there, having my mom say, 'The boys are working here, just let them do it,' and begrudgingly sitting there, trying to enjoy dinner, even before the wine glass fell off.

I could hear the conversation between him and my mom.

'How is David old enough to get this car?'

'Well, he's old enough to buy it, but we'll need to register it for him.'

At a later date, when I was sixteen and had my driver's license, my dad had to go out of town, and he was experiencing a problem with one of the pollution-control devices on his new company car—the catalytic converter. These things have a tendency to get clogged, which backs up the exhaust and stops the car from running. I guess he was heading to the airport and his CC was clogged up, and it wouldn't run, so he asked me to give him a ride in the Pontiac.

I said, 'Why yes, Dad, I'd be happy to,' and he got a hell of a ride, because my car was fast—probably much faster than I needed or should really have had at the time. That car would be out of my price range today, but back then I bought it for five hundred dollars. It was affordable because it was just a junky old car at that point. It needed some work but I was happy to do that because I enjoyed it.

I've always had friends who are into cars or bikes and like mechanical things. I love building motors and making things go fast. I currently have two Mercury Cyclones—one from 1970 and another from '72, although they had dropped the name Cyclone by the time the later one was built. These have large engines, which is the part I'm really into. I like cars to look a certain way, probably initially inspired by the *Mad Max* movies, but these are the closest American versions of the Australian Falcon. I like the lines; they're ominous-looking.

I get these oddball cars, which makes it more difficult for me if they need new body panels and such, because in the case of more popular vehicles, like Mustangs and Chevelles and Camaros, you can literally buy brand-new sheet-metal parts out of a catalogue. But with my cars, they didn't make that many of them to begin with, so I have to beg, borrow, and steal at swap meets and go through old junkyards out in the middle of nowhere and try to find parts for these vehicles—because the only way you're going to get a replacement item is to pull it off another car.

As time passes, more and more of these cars come out of

circulation. A lot of them were made in the heyday of Detroit's automotive boom, and a lot of them stayed local, which means that for six to eight months out of the year they're exposed to snow and ice and the salt that they put on the road, so they're all rust-buckets, and eventually they find their way to the junkyard. But I love them. I've always been into cars, ever since I can remember. I liked car movies, I liked racing—anything that had to do with fast motor vehicles. Not necessarily Formula 1—more NASCAR and American drag racing, funny cars with very high horsepower.

I still enjoy the sound of a well-cammed motor. There's nothing like the sound of an old-school push-rod big-block American V8 that's got a big lopey cam. The note of the exhaust is musical. Building a motor, putting it in the car, and starting it for the first time—and then having everything work as it should—is a magical experience.

Since that first 1968 GTO, I've had another Pontiac Le Mans, which is a lower version of a GTO with the same body style, and a really cool '68 Chevy step-side truck. This can be an expensive hobby if you really want to go fast, so as compulsive as I am, if I'm inspired by something that I've seen in a magazine, I'm liable to make a bad choice and go and buy some stuff that will get me worse fuel economy. If I was worried about fuel economy, none of my vehicles would be ideal. But they're just fun. I rarely drive them, apart from to car shows now and then.

When you build something with your own hands, you have a different relationship to it than to something that you just go and buy. Some people do that; they're not mechanically inclined, but they want the vehicle, so they go and spend a whole bunch of money on it. It probably costs more to do it myself, but I enjoy it; I want my hands to build those engines. I've also worked on friends' cars, just for the camaraderie.

I have a couple of motorbikes in the garage, and they're formidable. I had many motorbikes when I was a kid—small ones, for children, with a top speed of forty or fifty miles per hour. Some kids play football and baseball, some kids are into rock'n'roll and hot rods; I've just always enjoyed motorized vehicles. We'd go out on the trails and set up little jump ramps and have fun.

I had a makeshift go-kart when I was really young, which my dad made out of a lawnmower, and we souped it up. Most of my friends had motocross racing bikes, but my father never bought us mini-bikes because it was illegal to ride them on the street. Everybody did it anyway. I managed to get one from a friend of mine; it wasn't running, but I fixed it up, and we'd ride around and have fun.

Later, I went on to larger bikes. I was into high-performance sport bikes; I had a Suzuki GSX R-1100 that was really fast. Unfortunately, I found that when you have a bike that is capable of doing certain types of things, you want to do those things, and you end up doing really reckless driving. You do wheelies, and you find yourself weaving in and out of traffic, simply because the bike is designed so well and purpose-built for that. It's not safe, so you start having a few close calls here and there.

I had that Suzuki around the *Blessed Are The Sick* tour. I was living in an apartment at the time, and we were on tour just so damn much that it was sitting outside in the weather. I'd come home and try to get it started, flush the fuel system and push-start it and all this stuff, just to get it going again. There was a kid in the neighborhood who kept pestering me to sell it to him, and after I realized that the bike was being gradually ruined by being left out in the wet, I sold it to him.

I was bike-less for a number of years after that. I had to wait until I felt that I was beyond the point that I wanted another sport bike. I really felt like it was going to be the death of me. I still enjoy riding, I just don't feel the need to have a bike that is capable of making me feel like I want to drive like a madman. I wanted to outgrow that urge, because riding a bike is a little dangerous, especially in traffic. You need to be acutely aware of your surroundings, because when you're out and exposed, you need to be very cognizant of what traffic is around you. I prefer riding on country roads and back roads.

I have a Harley-Davidson now. I never saw myself having a bike with a trunk and a windshield—my car has those things, so what do I need a bike for? But a couple of my friends told me, 'You really ought to try this out. For three-day rides and whatnot, the level of comfort is incredible.' Anything you can do to eliminate rider fatigue is worth examining, so I rented one for a weekend and it was so comfortable, I felt like I was a passenger.

The biggest advantage for me is the reduction of turbulence when you have a windshield and you're riding at speed. Without one, you get beat up, especially if there are gusts of wind, too. If you do a three-hour ride at seventy miles per hour or more on a highway, you get a beating, and when you get to your destination you're not ready to party, you're ready to take a nap.

Of course, I've been down a few times and sustained a few injuries, just from getting a bit excited and going beyond what my capability—or that of the bike—can safely handle. Coming up on a blind corner on a sharp turn and having to take evasive action, for example—or in the rain, or if a car pulls out, and you have to do power slides through intersections. It just happens. Nobody likes it, and the older I get, the more it hurts, so I like to avoid these things at all costs.

Thankfully, none of my scrapes have resulted in broken bones, but I've busted myself up pretty good, mostly just road rash and bad bruises and swelling. It could have been worse; I have a lot of friends who had a lot of broken bones, and if they go through a metal detector they set it off, because they have plates and pins and so on. I'm grateful that that isn't my case. Then again, I outgrew my desire to ride like a hellion.

I always wear a helmet these days, no matter what, although we don't have a helmet law in Texas, where I live now, and nor did we have one when I lived in Florida. I'm not concerned about whether I look cool or not. I always wear boots and long pants, and as much gear as I can stand, given the heat of the day. I would never go out with shorts and flip-flops, like some idiots that I see.

There was a time around 1990 when I lost my car driver's license. I got a load of speeding tickets because I liked driving fast, and I didn't bother paying them. Clearly, this was a long time ago; I haven't had a speeding ticket in quite some time. My license was suspended, so I had to contact the local courts in the area out of state where the tickets were issued, and it was a mess.

I got pulled over in my car while my license was suspended, and the cop said, 'Sir, your license is suspended,' and I said, 'Really? I moved, here's my new address,' and he was like, 'I could take you to jail right now, but I'm gonna give you a pass. Take care of this,' because he was a nice guy.

That was when I sold my car and got the bike, which removed the problem. Of course, it rained all the time in Florida, which could be a little annoying at times, but that's just one of the stupid things you do when you're young and feeling rebellious. You could get a bike registered without having to have a driver's license or insurance. You could drive like a madman, and when the police try to pull you over, you just don't pull over, because they can't catch you when you have a fast motorbike. I lost them all the time.

I don't suggest for a moment that anyone reading this actually does this, but I fixed my license plate onto the bike with snaps rather than screws, and I tied a lanyard onto the side of it with a piece of wire, so if I found myself hauling ass and I saw a cop pulling out and trying to get behind me, I could reach behind me and slap the license plate. It would come off of the mount without me losing it and just flap about in the air, and the cop wouldn't be able to get a read on it.

Ordinarily, when the cops are going after a motorcycle, they just try to see what the plate is, and then they can catch you later, so I pulled that asset out of the equation. It was a bit of a James Bond thing to do, now I think about it. I'd whiz past them, they'd catch me on the radar and pull out and come after me, I'd see them, slap the plate, and take evasive action. When they realized that they couldn't see the plate, they'd give up. That was kind of funny. I was just testing the system, and I never got caught—on a bike, at least.

Nowadays, riding a bike is a relaxing thing for me, and more about getting out into nature and having the wind in my face and looking at the scenery. You can drive the same country road in a car, but it's a much different experience on a bike, because you're much more open and perceptive to your surroundings, which is really consistent with some of the things that I enjoy anyway.

I don't currently have bikes that do the kind of things that the early crotch-rockets, as we called them, did. Life is too short for that.

"I'm not really talking about cars and bikes here—they're just the context of the deeper meaning, which is my belief that transport, and thus travel, is good for the mind and for the soul. When your government betrays you, and your gods lie to you, why not reconnect with nature—ideally on a saddled-up Iron Horse?"

EYES TO SEE, EARS TO HEAR

FROM *DOMINATION*, 1995

Darkness swallowing all in its path
The blind leading the blind and the flock is ever confused
Who has the gift of healthy sight and mind?
Who can withstand while the others are blown away?

Eyes to see ... what the others see not
Ears to hear ... the voice of the elders guides
Eyes to see ... and the blind; they wither away
You fools! These eyes are never for you

Darkness corrupting all in its path
Greed leading the man to blindness, suffering
And ever foretold ... the meek shall have this earth
Alas, without sight they will only be left with demise

Worlds apart are they and I
My world remains in sight
Their lives despair
The I's and They's cannot compare

There is wisdom if you open your eyes to it, and this song challenges people to do just that. There's probably nothing more aggravating to me than when people don't use their wisdom to understand cause and effect. You throw a stone in still water and it sends ripples—so if you don't like the ripples, don't throw the stone. That seems very logical, but human beings often do things without considering the ramifications, and then they're surprised and say, 'Oh my goodness, I can't believe this happened!' Well, I *can* believe it.

Throughout history, there's probably a billion instances of this very thing: somebody taking action without thinking about the consequences. It's not just the action and the consequence, it's the lack of forethought and planning, even with the most minute of things. Once again, this brings us back to the simple truth that if folks just spent a bit more time harvesting and applying the knowledge of old, it would be helpful.

NOTHING BUT FEAR

FROM *DOMINATION*, 1995

Consequence … now the panic comes
You've dabbled in magik, your fingers are burned
Lost as you run towards the light
And deep in your heart you have nothing but fear

Your future is hanging by a strand
Your master makes his just demands
Game of life's price coming due
A swell of fear erupts in you

Your time is now!
Never a prayer, just silence rings
Charity works won't change a thing

Your balance of life is on our side
There's never a place to hide

What's so real is plain in sight
Cost to play: eternal life
For when we play, we play for keeps
Satan's marks forever we speak

Your time is now!
With screams you defy still silence rings
Prayers to some god won't change a thing
Gleam in your eyes reduced to tears
And deep in your heart you've nothing but fear

Why object to rewards, you know you've earned them
Why reject all your fantasy
You can't betray what your works have bargained for you
No use to fear what you have in store

Although some of the riffs in this song are a little complex, composing the lyrics was actually pretty easy for me. I was originally going to start it off quieter when it went into the main riff, but it's fine the way it turned out. In hindsight, it would have taken it into a direction that the band should not have been prepared to go in. I don't get too attached to things, though, so that was a really easy change to make, and I figured it out quick.

There are parallels with the story in this song to everyday life, with people doing things and oftentimes not thinking about the consequences, and then being surprised when there's an outcome that's not to their liking. History teaches us that there is virtually no situation that can't be resolved by drawing on previous knowledge about said situation. It may not be exactly the same, but it would be close enough. People do things and they're just surprised: *Oh, but how could that have happened? I thought that …* Well, frankly, my friend, you *didn't* think. This has happened as a result of something else.

It's not like it's difficult; it doesn't take a master to realize any of these things. It's just giving a little more thought and having your filters a little more in tune. People would avoid an awful lot of aggravation in life, just by employing the simplest tactics. It's shocking to me that we can be growing in so many different directions and enjoy so much of a technical revolution, even during my lifetime, and we're still just underneath the surface making the same damn emotion-driven mistakes that we have since the dawn of time. It's amazing how everything around us can continue to evolve—except us.

Regarding the line 'Deep in your heart you have nothing but fear,' it's easy to be reactionary-confident. It's not as easy to be confident when the ramifications of said actions come along, is it?

DAWN OF THE ANGRY

FROM *DOMINATION*, 1995

Cold finger on the trigger
Behind the line drawn in the sand
Anger rise!
We fight a war
With much at stake
The rights of birth
That no one can take

Overflowing with anger
Soon to be awakening
Will be martyrs on to glory
Dawn finds us in this rage

My finger on the button
With what's so foreign in my sights
Anger rise!
We wage a war … our nature to preserve
By any means … our enemies be gone

No longer can we wait
As an enemy drains our future
As the light of a new day shines
Our anger fuels our march this dawn

As it must be
Dawn of the mad

Call of duty now … all the minutemen rise and shine
Call of duty now … only sovereigns stand the test of time

My finger is on the trigger
Behind the line drawn in the sand

My finger is on this button
With what's so foreign in my sights

Anger rise!
We wage a war … our nature to preserve
By any means … our enemies be gone
No longer can we wait
As an enemy drains our future
As the light of a new day shines
Our anger fuels our march this dawn

As it must be
This dawn of the mad

This is a first-person song about the Gulf War, but not from a political standpoint, more of a personal one. I was putting myself in the place of a lone soldier who is watching an invading force come in, and asking myself what his motivation might be at that moment. How might someone feel in that position?

The metaphor extends to a nuclear button in the next verse. If you know the film *300*, and remember the scene where the small army is waiting in a tight spot for the much larger army to attack them, that would be a very close parallel to where my head was at when I was writing the song.

My feeling about the Gulf War is that I generally don't like these conflicts. The television is not going to convince me that it's our job to go in and fight someone who we've defined as a bad guy, just because that is the popular narrative. Is it the job of the US military to go in and change the environment and make it safe for multinationals to go in and, dare I say it, Americanize a place and put a McDonald's on every street corner and pave the way for business activities?

Regime change is not really something that is in my wheelhouse. If we have a problem with somebody, we should just isolate them. Don't have anything to do with them. It's a really a freedom thing: I don't like it, and I never have.

There's always more to the story than just one bad guy that we have to get rid of. The CIA and the military-industrial complex have roles behind the scenes that are not really talked about. It's like a magician's sleight of hand: they keep you occupied on one thing while all these other things are going on in the distance.

chapter seven

ONCE MORE MORBID

"Why return to a situation with the same old attitude? Go back with renewed strength, conviction, and confidence, or don't go back at all."

In the eight years since I left Morbid Angel, I'd listened to the albums that they'd recorded with their new singer, Steve Tucker, and I thought there was some good stuff there. The music was very different, as one would expect it to be. I went to a couple of Morbid Angel shows when they were in town, and actually Trey came over when they were planning their 2003 album, *Heretic*, and we discussed the idea of me working on that record.

I didn't feel that the timing was right, or that I was mentally prepared to do so, but it was a good conversation. I certainly considered it, but I was lukewarm about it, and lukewarm is a terrible temperature to be. In the absence of heat, there is only cold, so it was not right for me at the time.

By 2004, the band had done *Heretic*, and I guess they had done whatever touring they were going to do for that record. I got a call from Gunter, who said that they had a new tour booked. It had already been canceled once and rescheduled, and now it was going to be canceled yet again, for some reason.

He asked me how I would feel about doing four or five shows with Morbid Angel, so I thought about it, and I decided that it could be interesting. The gigs were only a couple of weeks away, though, so I asked him to consider that point, because I really wanted it to be good.

I discussed it with Gen prior to doing it, and she said, 'How do you feel about it?' I said, 'I don't know, but I think I can do it.' She was concerned about where I was at mentally, but she also thought it would be good for me.

So I went to meet Trey, Pete, and Tony Norman, who was the second guitarist at the time. I hadn't met him before, but he seemed like a talented guitar player. I didn't feel any weirdness at all; it felt like no time had passed. It was really enjoyable and a lot of fun. There was no negativity; it felt right, which was one of the motivators for me. I was in a much better place than I'd been back in 1995, of course, so I really walked in with a positive attitude, instead of the way I'd approached things before.

I went back and reviewed the songs, having discussed the setlist with the band, and there were a few moments on listening to the record when I thought, *Gosh, what did I play here?* But when we got into the rehearsal room, it all came back to me immediately.

As I walked into the room, I recalled what my mindset had been while I was performing the catalogue back in the nineties. Now, in 2004, I had a different take on it. It didn't come from a need to rage; I felt like I was beyond that. I felt the same energy, but that energy was now coming from a much less self-destructive point of view.

We started with a few shows in South America, which was always a very good market for the band. I remember the first night very clearly. When I set foot on the stage for the first time in Monterrey, Mexico, having not played with Morbid Angel for almost nine years, the roar of the audience was just deafening. I felt really good about it because everything from the past was just water under the bridge.

It was *time*.

The enthusiasm from the audience was off the chain. It was literally insane. I felt an overwhelming love from them, and I was being showered with it. This kind of reaction hadn't even been on my radar for a long while.

I hadn't ever thought that this reunion was going to happen, but I quickly started to realize how much everybody had grown.

Morbid Angel was obviously an important part of people's lives. Whether I had ever considered that fact—from my new attitude or my old one—I'm not sure. I don't think I had, but it was something that I was made very aware of now.

I was receptive to this now that I had gained empathy for people—not in an egotistical way, as previously it would have been. There was genuine love there, because people grew up listening to our music. The number of people who would come up to me and tell me this story or that about the power of our music helping them through tough times in life was huge. I really started to be able to relate to this, and empathize with some of the things they were telling me. That was really cool.

We were down there doing these shows, and it was one huge event after another. All of the shows were packed, and the people were really, really enthusiastic—to the point where they were singing along with every song, oftentimes louder than the PA, which would be drowned out. And I mean everybody—not just two or three people in the front row. The whole damn place.

We got back to the USA and said, 'Well, that felt pretty good.' Gunter said, 'I'm glad to hear it, because the booking agent's phone is ringing off the hook, from everywhere.' They were getting calls that they'd never gotten before, which I thought was a huge validation. Everybody felt good about it, and we all said, 'Yes, this feels right,' so we embarked on a whole lot of touring across the USA and Europe on this quote-unquote reunion tour.

Everything went really well, although this being Morbid Angel, there were speed bumps along the way. At one point, Tony disappeared and was unable to continue. I knew that he did drugs but I didn't know to what extent, because he kept it hidden from us, but the effects of this were that he would disappear for long periods of time. I guess when you pay people well, it enables them to spend money on their own issues. I'm not going to tell somebody what to do with their own time, but when it interferes with the prime reason that we're there, which is to give people value for money, then you need to step up. After all, people have all kinds of options of what to do with their hard-earned money, and if they're coming out and purchasing a ticket because they want to see a show, it's just rude not to give them one hundred percent.

Even in the old days I always felt that way—that I had a duty to myself and to everybody else to go out and give the very best, honest, hard-working performance I could, and be passionate about it. So, along the way, Tony disappeared, and we ended up not being able to get in touch with him. We had a festival in Portugal that we were booked on, and we ended up having to do it as a three-piece, because Tony had disappeared again. We got through it, but it didn't sound the same.

We realized that we needed to do something about the situation, and because I really wanted to work with Erik again, I called him up, although I almost felt bad doing it, because the guy had become so successful as a producer and studio owner. I said to him, 'I'd really like it if you would do this tour—it would be really cool,' and he did.

What had started off as a small thing turned into a worldwide phenomenon that everyone wanted to see. Enough time had passed so that our fans had grown older. I remember we were down in Chile, which was always a stronghold for us: we went there really early on, when General Pinochet was on his way out, around 1990. It was still a strict country at the time, with a military police presence.

I've had frank discussions with friends of mine down there, and I would attribute the fact of Chile being a stable and relatively safe country in a region that is filled with instability, and things that are not safe, as being traceable to the stricter government. My friends agreed with me, as much as people hated Pinochet and his violations of human rights.

We were playing there one night, and my tour manager came up and said, 'This girl really wants to talk to you, but I can get rid of her if you want.'

'No, it's cool,' I said.

She said, 'I just wanted to tell you that I had a really tough time when I was growing up. I considered all kinds of drastic things, but your songs spoke to me in a certain way. They emboldened me and gave me the strength to overcome a lot of obstacles that I had in my life, and I went to law school. Now I'm a partner in a major law firm, and I want to thank you for inspiring me.'

It was incredible: she was giving me credit for that. It caused me to pause and think.

The next day, also in Chile, this guy showed up backstage and told me a similar story: he owned three restaurants and invited us to come and have a meal on him. He kept the restaurant open late for us.

It turned out that of the kids who had listened to us the first time round, many of them had made successes of their lives, and from some of the stories they told us, I had been a big motivating factor in their lives. They also felt that it was important that they told me this.

That was humbling, and worth more to me than any check I've ever gotten from playing the biggest festivals in the world. I see that as making a real difference, rather than the self-aggrandizement of being a quote-unquote rock star. When an individual spills their heart out, and it's important for them to let you know that they attribute their motivation and their ability to overcome challenges to one of your songs, it doesn't get any better than that.

You hear people saying, 'You're a big influence on me,' and so on, and indeed I've said those things to musicians who I've looked up to since I was a kid, because I know what those artists have done for me—so to be able to pass down the gift that's been given to me is my drug, and it's better than any conventional drug you can think of.

I knew the members of Pantera well. I had become friends with their singer, Philip Anselmo, from playing shows—theirs and ours. Phil would always come to our shows and sing a song with me onstage. And Dimebag Darrell, their incredible guitar player, was a Genitorturers fan, and he would come to their shows, which is where I got to know him.

Dime and I used to drink together; if you were a friend of his, you didn't have a choice. He used to say, 'Drink it or wear it!' and hand you a drink. If you didn't drink it, he'd literally douse you with it, and then repeat it until you drank it. You could hang out with him for ten minutes and you almost felt that you were hanging out with your best friend. He was just that kind of person.

In the early hours of December 9, 2004, I got a call in the middle of the night from Dean Zelinsky, formerly of Dean Guitars. I kept weird hours, so getting a call at one or two in the morning wasn't unusual. I was at the studio, working. He said, 'Dime's been shot. I think he's dead.'

At first I thought this was a really sick joke, and I got angry, like, 'Dean, don't call me with this kind of shit,' but he said, 'No, I'm serious.' I semi-dismissed it anyway, but then I learned the details, and it was terrible. I was profoundly shocked.

People who live on the edge, in what could sometimes be considered a reckless fashion, obviously have more opportunity to lose their lives prematurely, whether it be due to alcohol or drugs or whatever. If someone had phoned me and said Dime was drunk and fell off the side of a building and broke his neck, I'd be sad about it, of course, but it wouldn't be at the same level as someone being murdered by some crazed individual.

It got me thinking about what some piece of shit will do, to take away a friend of mine and a friend of the world's. I started seeing that the negativity that I had worked to get out of my life was all around. The internet fosters a kind of really hateful vitriol, where people make comments about things, and it becomes a real cesspool of negativity. Having an arena like this that allows these sorts of things to fester is incredibly non-productive, and that's putting it nicely.

So this really concerned me. I had been in a band, after all, and I had left that band—and a lot of people were unhappy about that. Were there more of these kinds of people out there, prepared to do these crazy things? I remember being onstage after that and feeling a little uptight, and looking around. I was maybe a little paranoid about whether the security was tight.

Unfortunately, it just takes one bad apple to do something

that sends shockwaves through the industry and through a lot of people's hearts. I spoke to other musicians about it, and we asked ourselves who was next. They all told me, 'When we go on tour now, everything is different.'

The days of audience members stage-diving at our shows were over—that was evident. We started seeing signs everywhere that said 'no stage-diving,' because the clubs were proactively trying to stop people getting hurt. Morbid Angel really didn't like stage-divers anyway, and I don't like it either. I've always felt like the stage was our domain. It's not that we didn't want people to enjoy themselves, but they come up the side of the stage and run across the front, stomping on the guitar players' pedals and breaking shit. It's just disruptive of what we're trying to do. If you want to get onstage, go start a band—then you can be onstage.

I think we—all of us—can do better. We should think carefully about going online and making random anonymous comments about things. There's virtually no accountability on the internet, and I don't support any websites that provide an arena for vitriol and negativity.

It has nothing to do with whether I have thick skin or not; I've dealt with this stuff for over thirty years, so it's not news to me. People love you, people hate you; it's part of life. But this was a new level, and sadly not a new level of confidence and power, as my friends in Pantera phrased it. It was a new low.

That was a really rough time. When I went to Darrell's funeral, I remembered this jovial, jolly individual who always had something funny going on. He had such a good energy. Now, I was looking at this body lying in a coffin, and that was not my friend, because what was there was lifeless, not jovial, and the literal antithesis of my friend. It saddened me very deeply.

I couldn't imagine the pain that his brother, Vinnie Paul, was feeling, especially having witnessed it happen before his eyes. That has to leave an indelible mark—it left one on me, although I wasn't family, and I didn't witness Darrell's murder. I don't know if I can even imagine the pain and suffering that his family and loved ones felt.

It was a reminder, just as it was when Vinnie himself passed away in 2018, that we live in a world that is often out of control.

I ask myself what steps we can take to discourage behavior that could lead to this kind of tragedy. It has nothing to do with guns. The thought process of, *He was murdered with a gun? Then we need to outlaw guns*, doesn't add up. What we need to do is grow up and make sure that we understand the consequences of our actions.

That incident aside—and it was a major one—in 2004 and '05 I felt that I was on a good path. I was much more in control of my ego. Things did continue to upset me from time to time, but the way that I dealt with them made it clear that the days of throwing sandwich trays out of the dressing room were over. My development had come through me taking a step back and saying to myself, *These are the things I need to work on.* One at a time, I started to address them, even though it was painful at times.

I never talked to journalists about the therapeutic process that I had put myself through. It would have been impossible to explain my motives in a few sentences, so I simply told them that I had dealt with some personal issues. There was no short way to explain it. This is why it's such a release for me to write this book and set the record straight at last.

In 2005, we did a tour with Soulfly in the States. I had first got to know their singer Max Cavalera in the tape-trading days, before his band Sepultura recorded their early albums. There was a lot of great Brazilian metal coming out in those days, and we got a lot of albums from their label, Cogumelo. There was a compilation called *Warfare Noise*, and I really liked the band Sarcofago as well.

When we played in Sarcofago's hometown of Belo Horizonte, Brazil, for the first time in April 1991, at a venue that was like a soccer arena, I requested that they join us on the bill, because we were big fans of theirs, and they made it happen. I met the singer, Wagner Lamounier, who called himself Wagner Antichrist. He sounds like a monster on his records, but that couldn't be further from the truth; in fact, he's a professor, and very articulate and astute. He comes from a similar place to the one I was coming from, which was interesting. Their album *I.N.R.I.* was very to the point. Some of that stuff had a lot of venom in it, together with a lot of rebellion against religion, because the church is very strong in Latin America.

Max Cavalera's concept for the 2005 tour was *War Of The Worlds*, so we had a globe with a yin-yang symbol of Soulfly on one side and Morbid Angel on the other. The first night of the tour was at an outdoor venue, and it was packed. I was backstage, and I heard this beautiful flamenco acoustic guitar. I almost thought someone was listening to an Ottmar Liebert CD or something, and I walked around the corner, and there was Soulfly's guitarist, Marc Rizzo, who I hadn't met before, working on music. It was truly beautiful, and he's a really nice guy, too. That was my first introduction to Soulfly. It was really inspiring. The tour was great, with excellent attendance, and two nights in some cities.

On the subject of guitarists, Erik Rutan had joined us for a really successful summer festival tour in Europe after Tony Norman left. I liked working with Erik because he was a really good guitar player, and also a team player. He told us that he'd be happy to help out again whenever we needed him, which we appreciated. However, his studio was so successful that we couldn't compete with it financially; by touring with us, he was actually losing money.

Erik was still willing to do it for us, because he was and is a good friend, but were we really being good friends in return by asking him to do us a favor that was not necessarily in his best interests? I didn't feel good about that, even though he is a super-talented guy who knows what he's doing.

When he left the band the first time, Erik really took it upon himself to achieve something, which he did first through Hate Eternal and then through the many albums he recorded at Mana Studios. I'm really proud of him.

I applaud people's success, and I know a lot of people who are multimillionaires and way more successful than I am. I'm not jealous of success; I'm supportive. I don't look at someone and think, *That guy has more money than me. Fuck him!*—although a lot of people do have that exact attitude. They hate it and think that somehow it's not fair. Personally, I think it's totally fair when people find ways to succeed, and I encourage it. I also study it and ask, *What approach did that person take toward their success?* and I consider whether that approach could be incorporated into some of the approaches that I have toward things.

At the end of the day, these things are always worth a try. Successful people can be good role models. If you get out there and get things done, I admire that. Whether or not I like them as individuals is not necessarily relevant. I look at people like Steve Jobs and Richard Branson, who had a vision to do something and conquered, and they did really well and employed a lot of people.

When people are successful, they're often philanthropic, and that's a really good inner motivator as well. People should look beyond their jealousy and admire someone who's successful and aspire to be that way, and then maybe take a few plays out of their playbook, whether it's a major change or just subtle things that you pick up.

I learned a lot from Elliott Rubinson of Dean Guitars, who died in 2017. He was a really successful guy, and I was a fly on the wall during some tough business conversations that he had, which spawned some thoughts that I had never had before. Generally speaking, these are the kinds of things that help me grow on a daily basis.

Of course, if you're in an internationally touring band, there are enough obstacles and hindrances in a given day to make your character broaden at light speed. One such thing comes to mind from July 2008, when I was arrested in Italy and charged with a weapons offense.

After Italy, we had a show in Greece to get to, and we didn't have time to take the land route, so we decided to drive to Milan and then fly to Greece, while the bus would drive on and pick us up when it got there the following day. So we were at the airport, and it was like any other time that I've flown. We had all our stage gear in checked bags, along with guitars and everything else, and sent it through the baggage conveyor.

Suddenly there was some security person who said, 'Mr Vincent?' and I said, 'Yes?' and he said, 'We have a question about your bags, could you come with us?' I followed him to a room full of armed military police, where I was arrested and handcuffed.

They told me that I had illegal munitions. I asked them what they were talking about, so they brought in my chrome bullet belt. These look like bullets, but they're just bullet casings with no primer or gunpowder inside them, so they're harmless. I remember one time when I was flying to the States from Heathrow in London, a security guy told me, 'You can't take this belt on the plane—they're weapons,' and I said, 'Do you even know what you're talking about?'

One of the armed police who patrol the airport was nearby.

I said, 'Hey, buddy, can I borrow you a second?'

He said, 'Yeah, what's up?'

I handed him the bullet belt and said, 'Can you have a look at this and explain to your colleague that this is not ammunition?'

He took one look at it and said, 'No firing pins, no gunpowder—it's fine.'

Everything was all right after that.

You just need to know what you're talking about in these situations, and yet the Italians were really serious about this. Meanwhile, the plane was getting ready to leave, and they told me to call the American consulate.

I said, 'What do I need to call the consulate for? It's a fucking stage costume!' but they just weren't having it. I had to give it up and get an Italian lawyer to post bond so I could make it to the damn show.

Now, if I'd just signed the bullet belt away, I could probably have made all this go away, but as it had come this far I was pissed off, and I wanted to make a damn point about it. If we were already doing this, I wanted it to go before a judge, and so it did.

Thankfully, I was able to arrange it with my attorney so that I didn't have to fly back to Italy to stand trial. At one point it seemed as if I was going to have to do that, but it was rightfully dismissed with prejudice. The judge really scolded the police about what they had done, and I was given what was effectively a 'get out of jail free' pass, which I could pull out next time I was traveling, to stop this kind of nonsense.

The easiest and cheapest way out would just have been for me to sneak out of there and not make a big deal of it, but they chose to make it a big deal. I was thinking about the next band that comes through, who maybe wouldn't have the means to fight this kind of nonsense to the extent that I did. I also wanted to prove a point, because I felt that I was right. It cost me six thousand euros—around seven thousand dollars—to get this done.

I got my bullet belt back, too, but it wasn't about the belt. I could easily get another one of those. It was about the notion that these things can happen. As soon as I got off the plane in Greece, a friend of mine took me to a shop where I bought another one for the show. These things are readily available—they've been a staple of heavy-metal culture since forever.

According to the paperwork from my lawyer, the Italian police were well reprimanded and hopefully deterred from doing these things anymore. But how often are there injustices that will simply continue if good people don't stand up and take the perpetrators to task? It's an abuse of power.

It's no secret how I feel about governmental intrusion into citizens' lives. I knew I had done nothing wrong, so I wasn't scared—I was just pissed off. I was like, *Okay, if we're going down this path, let's continue down this path*. I needed to see it through, not least because it was connected with my chances of ever getting into Italy again. And I did, and thankfully it was dismissed and all turned out well, other than I was out the six thousand euros that I would much rather have spent on something else. That could have been a new project hotrod right there.

Anyway—metal is clearly not fashionable in the fashion center of Europe. We only made it to the plane because we made a point of showing up early at airports, in case of bullshit like this.

A more pleasurable opportunity for artistic growth came later the same year, when Max Cavalera got in touch again. Max was recording Soulfly's album *Conquer* near Orlando and asked if I would be willing to make a guest appearance. I said yes, of course. Over the years I've been asked to do an awful lot of stuff, and sometimes the timing isn't right or I'm not into it, so, more often than not, I have not participated—but I was really into Max's idea, because it was really interesting.

The way that Max works is way different from the way that I've worked in the past. We started working on a song, and he had an idea of how he wanted it to go, so I had a go at it. When we came to the final part of the song, I asked him, 'What are you doing with this?' He said, 'I don't know yet,' so I said, 'I have an idea, and I'm happy to share it with you,' because I could hear the music without being close to it.

I said, 'It would lend itself to a slight arrangement change, if we can just do a quick mockup.' They had an engineer who was a really good editor, and he was able to put this thing together that I was asking for. I sat down to work, but then all these people came to visit and wanted to do a few shots and whatever. I said, 'Yes to all of that, but let me get this thing done first,' and then, 'All right, Max, here's what I'm thinking, let me just demo it for you. It's okay to say no, this is your album—I'm just trying to bring something to the table that I think you might like.'

He did like it, and it became the song 'Blood Fire War Hate' on *Conquer*. We were of like mind, so I ended up contributing more than the initial role that they had conceived. It was very organic and natural, and it ended up being the single for the record. It came out really well. I was just happy to be a part of it, because Max and I have been friends for so long, and I put as much into it as I would want to put into anything, or that I would like someone else to put into a project of mine, should I ask them to contribute. That's my standard modus operandi.

Talking of heavy-metal compadres, I got to meet Rob Halford of Judas Priest in 2009. Rob was living in Phoenix, Arizona, and our friend J.J.—who was one of the members of Rob's band Fight—also lived there, and he was always at our shows. I would suggest that he bring Rob, but J.J. always told me that Rob didn't go out much.

One time we rolled through Phoenix and I said to J.J., 'So, did you bring Rob?' I was expecting the answer to be no, but he said, 'Yes, he's standing outside the bus, but he doesn't want to bother anybody.'

I said, 'Dude, what the hell?' so Rob came up and said hello. He was a really polite, cool guy. I was thinking, *I grew up listening to this man*. After that, I'd see him at festivals, where everybody would be yelling at him, but he would always stop and say hello. He is a really nice English gentleman, and he never lost that. Who could call themselves a fan of metal and not appreciate the greats like Judas Priest?

The same is true of Iron Maiden—the great stalwarts of metal. We played a couple of shows with them at the MaidenFest event in Mexico. It was us, Carcass, Lauren Harris, and a Mexican band or two, and then Atreyu, who were not well received at all. The fans were very vocal and physical about the fact that they did not like that band. We went over well, fortunately, and Carcass went over great.

Bruce Dickinson is an excellent frontman. People don't realize how difficult it is to tour and be a vocalist, especially when you're trying to deliver an album-perfect performance every night. That's a lot of work. No part of being a vocalist is easy, because your instrument is subject to a whole host of conditions that wouldn't affect a guitar player, for example, who can still play if they have a sore throat.

We need to be on top of our hygiene, too, which can be difficult when you're in close proximity to a lot of people and shaking hundreds of hands—especially when it's cold and you're prone to catching a virus. I started getting a flu shot whenever I went on tour, and that really kept a lot of these things at bay.

Still, there have been times when I couldn't play a show, and it has killed me not to be able to do so, because the disappointment to people is huge. We were once scheduled to play a show in Greece, and I was not feeling well—and when I woke up on the day of the show, I could barely even talk. My tonsils were swollen, so I had a doctor come over, and he said, 'Cancel the show.'

To try and get through this, I slept as much as I could. I kept waking up and turning the shower on full blast and breathing steam. Ultimately, I got up onstage and told the crowd, 'I'm not even supposed to be here, but we're gonna do this!'

It was real rough, but I got through it. Was it the stellar performance that I would have liked to have delivered? No, but people appreciated it. I'm always really hard on myself, because I always want to be the very best that I can be. Sometimes these factors are beyond my control, and, as you know by now, I don't like that.

After Erik Rutan left the band, we needed to find another guitar player, and his replacement was going to have to be a really good musician—and also the right kind of person. We weren't thinking about recording any new music yet, because we were so into the reunion tour, which lasted three or four years. Fans didn't start asking that question for some time, because their reaction was still, 'Wow, they're back!' And we played a *lot*.

As I said, the first handful of shows led to a tidal wave of interest, and everything went back to the way it was originally, in terms of how the business was run and how profits were split. It's always been a laissez-faire relationship in that Gunter handled all the business and we would handle the music.

Gunter always did great work and kept his eyes open, which was important in this rather dishonest industry. Promoters have tried to cheat us many times throughout my career, but if they don't commit to paying you for your show, the solution is simple. If it looks like there's going to be a problem, then you find ways to address it *before* you play, when you still have some leverage. That's the number one way around those things. If they're stalling us, then we'll say, 'Well, we'll be on the bus, let us know when you want us to go on.' It's a two-way street. When you're a business owner, you're always the last to get paid. It's all part of an equation, and the equation has to be complete. I never want to cancel, and there have been very few times when that's happened, but it's a bummer when it does, because I'm amped up and I want to do the show.

Everybody contributed in the way that they were best suited to do so. Because of where I stood in the practice room, I usually directed the rehearsals, working in the new guys. This came to pass when we opened up auditions for a new guitar player. We didn't just want to find someone locally; we wanted the best candidate that we could get, so we sent out the word and told guitarists who were interested to learn the same three songs and to send us a video in which their hands were clearly visible.

'The charts for the songs that are on the internet are wrong, so listen to the songs and show us what you've got,' we told them.

I was the one getting the videos, and there were a lot of them. Some of them weren't even close; some were more interesting. We got it down to six guitarists, all of whom were capable of doing the job and were people from other bands that you may have heard of. I brought those six videos down, and Trey and Pete and I reviewed them all and discussed them.

Some of the guys played wrong notes here and there, but that had been part of the task—to listen to the records, go on YouTube, and figure out the songs. We wanted to see how people could do that, as part of the whole package, because if I was going to give guitar lessons, I didn't want to have to go through every little thing and be a guitar teacher.

They were all qualified, but I thought Thor 'Destructhor' Myhren from the Norwegian bands Zyklon and Myrkskog was the best suited, although I didn't reveal that opinion to the other two until they'd seen all six. I didn't know this, but in the years of my absence, Morbid Angel had actually played with Zyklon, so they already knew Thor.

We made our decision and arranged to give Thor a call, which I did at a time that I guess was the middle of the night over in Norway. He thought that I was calling with condolences, but I said, 'Congratulations!' and he said, 'Really?' He was extremely happy and thankful. I said, 'Why are you thanking me? I didn't play guitar, you did.' He had earned his spot through his own talent.

Thor continued to live in Norway, but he would come over and stay for long periods, either with me or with our engineer, Juan 'Punchy' Gonzalez, who has sleeping quarters at his studio for the bands who record there. (Punchy first got that nickname when he started working for the band as Pete's drum tech. He had really long, curly hair, and he used to tie it up and put it on the top of his head. The crew reckoned that he looked like the mascot for the drink Hawaiian Punch, whose name was Punchy. The nickname stuck.)

Thor worked really hard, and it was fun having him in the band. He's a really funny guy, and he became affiliated very quickly to the band's sense of humor. He got it really quickly, although he is definitely very Norwegian. We were truly becoming an international band, because we had a Central American drummer, a Scandinavian guitarist, and a couple of regular old Americans.

We did a fair amount of touring together, and then we started working on the new record. 'Nevermore' was the first new song that we wrote, and it went over really well. We played it live before the time came that we decided to record the new album. But before that could happen, we lost our drummer.

I remember Pete saying, 'My back is killing me' over the years, but I don't think any of us realized that his injuries were as severe as they were. He pushed himself really hard when he was playing drums. I know a number of drummers who have experienced a lot of joint issues and muscular discomfort, like sports injuries. If you beat on stuff, you take a beating. We've all been through it: I've been through some neck issues myself.

Then again, when people complain about stuff, you assume they're crying wolf. Everybody does it if they're just upset about something. You blow up and complain about this, that, and the other thing. Some of that is just to kill time when you're on tour—like, *Man, this food sucks!* You just dwell on negativity because you woke up on the wrong side of the bed. So although Pete was in a lot of pain, I don't think any of us realized how bad it was.

In all honesty, being in Morbid Angel was always a difficult job for a drummer. It's not easy to play this stuff. Pete would come down and we'd rehearse new stuff and try out new things, but it was going slow, because he was in pain. I'd ask him what was wrong, and he'd say it was his back, so I would say, 'Let's stop and take a break,' or, 'Let's not do any more tonight; let's pick it back up tomorrow.'

He would come in the next day and still be really sore, though, so we would take the next three days off. We were unaware of how serious the situation was, but then he had an MRI done, and the results were really bad—to the point where, if he kept pushing it without doing anything about it, he would potentially become disabled. He had multiple herniated discs, some of which were leaking.

Pete was always such an athletic guy, which was the reason for his high-speed, articulate playing. When he was playing double bass he pushed really hard, which was constantly pounding on him. His injuries were like sports injuries, which was appropriate, given that he was approaching fifty and had been doing this for a long time. You don't see football players out there at fifty years old, doing what they did when they were in their twenties.

We knew we needed to get after this, because Pete was in so much pain. We tried really hard, taking off as much time as we could. I told Pete to rest his back as much as he could, and not to lift heavy things and exacerbate the situation. With the new songs, we would get them more or less where they needed to be, but then his back would give out. Then we would get back together three or four days later and try to get back to the point we'd reached.

We understood it now; there was a very real chance that Pete would end up in a wheelchair if he kept on pushing the drums the way they needed to be pushed. Still, we knew people who said, 'Why are you doing this to Pete?' and we'd reply, 'Quite the contrary—we're doing our best for him.' Other people would ask us how rehearsals were coming along, and we'd say, 'They're not.'

One day, Pete just said, 'Guys, you need to find someone else. I can't do this.' It was not what I wanted to hear, but he couldn't do it anymore—and this was coming from him. It wasn't as if we said, 'Pete, you need to do this or you're going to get replaced.' He actually came to us. I said to him, 'Do you understand what you're saying?' and he said, 'I do.'

So Pete was out. In 2012, prior to having back surgery, he flew out to Los Angeles and recorded the drum tracks for a whole host of Terrorizer songs with a new singer and guitar player. He asked me if I would be willing to play on the record. I said, 'Sure, dude,' even though it wasn't particularly profitable, because he had asked me if I would do this for him.

No good deed goes unpunished, and he got really sore at me for whatever reason. It ended up not ending well, but I recorded the bass tracks and turned them over. There was some drama, and I'm not a dramatic person, so that's where it ended for me.

There is a really limited number of drummers who can handle Pete's drum parts. There were plenty of drummers who could play fast, of course, but that's not the same thing at all. The first person I spoke to was George Kollias of Nile, because I knew that he could do it.

We had a number of discussions about it. He said, 'I'll learn the songs and I'll play on the record the way that Pete would do it,' but I thought that we needed someone to do the record and then commit to at least a certain amount of the subsequent touring.

George certainly could have covered it, and I thought we could offer him an appropriate salary, but I didn't allow myself to think that, because Karl Sanders is a friend of mine, and I wouldn't do that to him. I told George this, and I asked him to recommend some names. I also asked Erik Rutan, who suggested Tim Yeung as a capable drummer.

I mentioned this to George, who said, 'Tim would be an excellent choice. He could do it.' So I got on the phone with Tim, who I didn't yet know, and asked him if he would be interested. He said, 'Fuck yeah! I grew up listening to Pete, man.'

Tim came in and played, and his style and feeling were considerably different to Pete's. He could play Morbid songs with no problem, and they sounded a bit different but still good. I showed him one of the new songs and asked him how he would play it, and at that point he took ownership of the role and played really well, with excellent timing. So he came in and we got the set down for some live shows that we had coming up, as well as working on the new material.

The new album, *Illud Divinum Insanus*, generated a lot of discussion on its release in 2012. Here's what went down. A lot of the demos that Trey brought in at the beginning of the rehearsals reflected the fact that he's really into dubstep and techno, which is really strange stuff. The way the songwriting worked on previous albums was that Trey would sit down with a drum machine, put some riffs down, and then say to the rest of us, 'Here's the song idea, and here's how it goes.' We'd work on it and get it where it needed to be, thinking about vocals and making some arrangement adjustments here and there, and we'd set up the song to where the verses and choruses were perfect.

For *Illud*, the process was different. Trey had weird mixtapes on which he had mashed stuff together, and he said, 'This is what I'm trying to get.' I listened to it, and at first I didn't know what the hell I was listening to. I'd say things like, 'What is the guitar part you're hearing here?' because he was really experimenting with something different. This was way beyond the Laibach collaborations we'd done, for instance. It was very strange stuff.

He was saying, 'We'll put additional electronic trigger pads as part of the drum set,' so I asked him what he heard as the snare, and how we could take this mash-up and turn it into something that could actually be done in the room with bass, guitar, and drums.

Everything that is on the record is played. Nothing is programmed, other than the 'Omni Potens' march, which I did on a keyboard at the beginning. Tim played all the drums, just with different sound sources. Not everything is to a perfect click, either—some of it moves around.

It was really difficult; we spent months down there, literally every day, listening to Trey playing a riff and trying to figure out how we could take his vision from the really weird-sounding tape that he'd brought in and turn that into a song.

At first I thought, *I don't know … this doesn't necessarily sound like Morbid Angel to me*, but at the same time, Morbid has always sounded like a lot of different things, so I was really excited about it.

It was really weird, but I like really weird stuff anyway. I like Voivod, I like Pink Floyd, I like strange music, so I thought it might be a new sound. I was all about going for it, just because it was weird and strange and unexpected and unpredictable.

Trey wrote six songs, and we recorded the drums for those with Erik at his studio, and Trey then went back and did all these edits on those songs. Again, he wanted them to sound like the mash-up tapes he had originally brought in. It was difficult to know what the end point would be, but he heard something, and I could tell that he was on the verge of something. I wanted to be supportive of that, because I thought it might be something new.

Trey then worked with Punchy on the guitars. I walked into the control room, and there was every kind of effect pedal on the floor that I've ever seen, as well as some that I'd never seen before. He was using them to get strange sounds and allow him to figure out what the guitars were going to be.

In the meantime, Tim and I went to a different studio to record drums for the other four songs on the record. When I came back, Trey was like, 'Hey, man, listen to this!' I knew he was on to something, so I said, 'Just continue what you're doing,' and he spent a couple of months on one-hundred-plus tracks and track management.

After that, I came in and listened to what was going on. I played what was appropriate for my instrument and then sat back with a rough instrumental and wrote my parts to go across the top of it. I really had no idea at that point what the end result was going to be.

Trey finally got to a point where, after two months of just beating his head in, he said, 'I can't do any more.' We still had four songs to do, two of which were written by Thor, so because I could tell at that point that Trey was done, I said, 'We can get these songs done. If you want to come in, you can, if you feel up to it.'

Thor had written his two demos with a drum machine and sent them over from Norway; I added lyrics, and Tim and I rehearsed them, just the two of us. There was something on the demo where there was a weird flub on the drum machine that we knew wasn't supposed to be there, and it created this very odd timing, so we found a way to include that, which was really neat.

When Thor came in, he played guitar to our parts, and he said, 'Oh, man, you guys really did a good job.' Tim really nailed the drum parts, and we filmed him recording it. That guy worked his ass off. He was so on top of his game—he just bludgeoned those songs. He has a lot of finesse, and a sort of cockiness to his playing, almost in an old Cozy Powell kind of way, and he would actually windmill his head while playing drums.

People would always razz Tim about his showmanship, but I'm used to playing with drummers who are a little bit showy—I think it's fun. I like to watch a drummer who is showy, because it's part of the visuals of the show, but I've never seen somebody be able to spin sticks and do big arena-rock moves while playing at 260 beats per minute. Sometimes we'd play it up live, simply because he had the ability to do it.

Tim can do spontaneous things really easily, so we had our communication set up really well live. I always wore chrome tips on my boots, so my signal to him if I couldn't hear something was to turn my boot sideways and bounce where I thought the beat was. This would let him know what I was thinking. I don't want to think about timing, because I'm spinning plates up there—singing, playing bass, and addressing the audience—so if something weird happens, you don't have time to find out what's wrong. If there's an issue, it needs to be solved really quickly, without breaking my concentration. It's neat to be able to communicate nonverbally, and Tim responded to that really well.

When aggressive, extreme metal is tight and articulate, it's totally badass. When it's not, it's a complete train wreck. That line is real thin, so it was always a challenge to get everybody to revisit a song and perform it at a certain tempo. We needed to have things that breathed a bit and sounded good, not just fast stuff all the time.

We didn't play to a click, either. I've played with drummers who play with a click live, and it really hinders spontaneity, because everything is exactly the same. I record vocals to a click, though, because I want to make sure that I get that snap. I like to sing off and around the beat as well.

Illud was mixed by Sean Beavan, a producer who has done a lot of great albums, and I recorded some vocals at his house. We were right up against a NAMM show that year, so I worked as much as I could—but I didn't want to do too much. Three or four hours of screaming is about right per day for me; that means I'm not pushing my voice too hard, and I can do it again the next day. In the past, I've pushed it so it hurt. That happened during *Covenant*, and I had to take a week of voice rest. It hurt bad.

Sean sent out mixes for our approval, although I was the only one who was making comments. I don't know why Trey didn't chime in. Maybe he didn't listen to it; maybe he was just burned out at that point. I think he'd just run out of gas and thought, *I've done all I can do*. Later, he complained a lot about the record, but if he'd commented at the time when we were mixing the album, perhaps it would have turned out differently.

It seemed to me that he'd washed his hands of it, even though I'd sat down with him for months, helping him to realize his vision; the least we could do was see it through to fruition. That seemed weird.

Looking back at *Illud*, I worked as a team member on what seemed to be the demo-direction style. One of the songs that I wrote, 'Radikult,' started off in a completely different direction. I altered it to make it more in line with what I felt was going to be indicated by Trey. I took what I had to work with, went in, and put the most passionate feeling into every vocal on that record—way more than I ever have, and that's undeniable.

In hindsight, would it have been better for me to say, 'Well, Trey, let's go in a different direction'? And would his attitude to me then have been, 'Well, you're just not supportive of anything new'? I don't know. Anything is speculation, and hindsight is 20/20. Do I think that there could have been a few more 'Nevermore's and a few less 'Too Extreme!'s? Yes, but that's not the way it came out. It didn't work that way.

Initially, there was a lot of backlash about *Illud*, but then initially there was a lot of backlash about *Blessed Are The Sick* as well. And when we did *Covenant*, there was a lot of backlash about 'God Of Emptiness.' Some of the reviews were really good, some were mixed, and some were downright bad—not even to the point where they could appreciate the things that could be considered 'traditional' Morbid Angel songs. They wanted to go straight after what they didn't like.

Everything is an acquired taste; Morbid Angel were an acquired taste from the very beginning. The interesting thing to me is that when we did *Blessed*, everybody was like, '*Altars* was so much better—they slowed down.' As the years went by, I started hearing people say, '*Blessed* is my favorite record,' because when something is different, it takes people a while to get up to speed with where things are.

To that end, a lot of people have told me that initially they didn't like *Illud*, but now, as they listen to it more, they get it, and they really like it. That was my thought all along; that there would be some people who didn't like it at all. Because we're in such a super-quick-turning cycle, the amount of time that people take to savor an album is short. People's attention span in the world we're living in today is much shorter, so they're on something and then off of it fifteen minutes later and on to something new, because there's so much going on and because there are so many things that are vying for our attention.

I was even prepared to take a couple of the *Illud* songs and put them into the set in a way that was more suitable for a live version. We discussed that, but it never came to fruition. For example, 'Too Extreme!' is a bit long, but its essence is pretty manic, and the drums are really interesting. Any of these songs could have been brought into a live environment, and they would have been a nice part of the overall portfolio.

Again, it doesn't matter, because I know what people are going to want to hear—'Maze Of Torment,' 'Immortal Rites,' 'Fall From Grace,' 'Rapture,' pretty much all of *Covenant*, and most of *Domination*. Those are what people love, so even though they know you've got a new record out, they still shout for 'Immortal Rites.'

It's the same for any band. Ozzy Osbourne has a million albums out, but do you think he'll ever be able to go onstage and not play 'Paranoid'? This is just the way it works. People have their favorite things, and they want to hear the greatest hits.

I think the album is good. Some of it is very different from what people would expect from us, but I will tell you this: there's a whole group of people that became fans of the band that weren't fans previously—as was the case when we did 'God Of Emptiness.' That one song brought in an entirely different demographic of Morbid Angel fans.

I have wide musical tastes, too, but it starts with metal and rock and stringed instruments. I listen to some hip-hop and I hear some interesting elements that sound cool, but, man, does that make it right for Morbid Angel? A lot of the fans didn't get it. Maybe they were expecting something that sounded like something we had done before. So many bands these days do just that.

In retrospect, I realize that we've always done weird stuff and strange things on our albums—maybe for the last song on a record, or an interlude between tracks. This time, though, there was a lot of that kind of material. It wasn't buried in the back of the record.

I certainly did my part to make my contributions to *Illud* as deep as I've ever done on anything. Ultimately, only the band can accept ownership of something; people can decide that it's more expedient to point fingers, but each of us have to point fingers at the fellow in the mirror. I just did my part in that. Let's see if others are able to do the same.

We also issued a remix album for *Illud*; we had discussed it, and we wanted to do it. Trey was really big on it. He probably would have preferred a lot of the original album to sound that way, as he was really into this kind of dubstep, so we discussed it with the label. I suggested a few people that I'd like to see on the list, Trey gave his list, and the label had ideas, too.

I said, 'Let's turn this into an art project—I don't want to direct it. Let's just see what people come up with and what they pick up on, which songs they want to do.'

There are multiple versions of different songs. Some of it is really interesting to me and some of it is complete shit, but that's okay—it's an art project for which we supplied the material for other artists to interpret as they chose. What people picked up and what direction they went in was really interesting to me.

Regardless of the critical reaction to our latest music, Trey didn't seem happy. It got to the point where I simply focused on doing my job to the best of my ability every night. It was painful for everyone, especially on the last tour.

Trey and I spoke on the phone on June 18, 2015. He said, 'Listen, man, we can't work together any more.' I asked him what he meant, and he said, 'That last record, whatever it was supposed to be, it would have been better if either you hadn't been there or I hadn't been there.'

I didn't understand that comment, and he didn't elaborate. He seemed resentful toward me, and that was how Morbid Angel—in terms of my musical involvement, at least—ended. I asked our fans not to take sides, because there was no need for that to happen.

I was slightly annoyed with the way this scenario unfolded—

although not as annoyed as I had been by the terrible energy between Trey and me on those last few tours. Mostly I felt a sense of liberation, in the same way that taking a dump after a period of constipation makes you feel better. I was straddling the fence between sour and fresh, and in this sense I was ready for change. It ended up being ideal motivation for new chapters in my life.

The last Morbid Angel activity in which I was involved was a live vinyl LP, *Juvenilia*. Earache came to us and said, 'Record Store Day is coming, and we have this show that we recorded back on your first tour at Rock City in Nottingham,' and I thought it was a great idea. It sounds really raw and honest—and it's juvenile, hence the name, which was Trey's idea. It was perfect. We were just forging ahead at the time, with a whole bunch of brand new experiences coming at us very quickly.

I felt the same way in the summer of 2015. New avenues were opening up for me, and, after thirty years of being a professional musician, I felt as though I was just beginning on my creative journey.

“Life is all about evolution, and when obstacles come your way, you can treat them either as a threat or as an opportunity. I always choose the latter. The value lies in how we choose to grow through these encounters.”

THIS MEANS WAR

FROM *DOMINATION*, 1995

Savagery, as judgment days arrive
Long we have waited for this time
How many brothers fallen?
How many kept alive as slaves for the wicked few?
'Tis time for reparations
'Tis time to settle scores
This time we give no warning … this means war!

Savagery, 'tis now our spirit overflows
War, our minds are focused, we are one
Hear now the winds of change
A force to obviate
All the enemies naked now
All the smoke gone and all their mirrors are broken
Lost empires crumble; destiny
Behold! I crusader, no retreat

Years of complacency on the part of the mob
Feeding on lies … so slothed, so full this is it
Restless … and tolerance nearing its peak
Woe to the next ones who push us to far

Our love is now replaced by war
Live cannot be spared, our victory at hand
And by my hand I slay the first

And the last will follow as we watch these wickeds bleed
No rest for the soldiers 'til the purge is done
No salvation until we drench this earth

The *Domination* period of my career with Morbid Angel was in some ways my highest point and in some ways my lowest, from an attitude standpoint. I felt that it was my best performance thus far, in terms of both songwriting and delivering the songs onstage.

At that point I was in full-on attack mode. I feel like I've definitely grown away from that person quite a bit since then, so trying to imagine exactly where I was at that point is not easy. Looking back and being objective is hard for me because separating myself from this time is so difficult, as it was so much a part of me.

If somebody asks me for my thoughts on a song they're writing, that's real easy for me to do, because I'm not attached to it at all. Songwriting is just a continuum that encompasses different stages of life. The more you experience, the more you have to talk about, right?

CAESAR'S PALACE

FROM *DOMINATION*, 1995

Just close your eyes … can you remember
The generations not so long ago
I feel the shameless urge that we must restore
Our former king to his rightful throne
And with me lords and maidens
We wait for the chosen son's return

I come alive
It's a time for celebration
Our will to restore
Make our past become the future once more

Still he lives! Two thousand years have passed
And still we're yearning for his return
We fulfill a wishful prophecy
And so the chanting begins
Hail Caesar … Hail Caesar … we render unto you
What is still yours

Share the wish as it must be
Our king and palace … mote it be!
Gods enslaved, traitors burning
Might and splendor forever return

I had picked up a video of *Caligula*, the 1979 movie, and the song is written from the perspective of a dream state about if that film was where we were today. I put myself in the first person and went into that world. I enjoyed the film immensely: there's some stuff in there that is a little objectionable, but sometimes it takes things that are objectionable in order to prove a point.

For example, there's loads of objectionable stuff in the Marquis de Sade's material, but once you get through that and you've thickened your skin enough to deal with it, you realize the amazing philosophy and social commentary that surrounds it. There's a lot of questioning and a lot of anti-religious thought in his work, too, which is both deeply thought-out and creative. The pornographic content is essentially elevator music compared to de Sade's underlying points.

INQUISITION (BURN WITH ME)

FROM *DOMINATION*, 1995

Come burning … are you going to burn with me
Won't you come burning … the world is watching
All the king's men riding hard
All their horses foaming
And if they were to catch us we'd be set ablaze

Burn!

Won't you come burning … all the dissident ones
Come and walk the line and you will burn with me
Witches yes, slaves never … and still I speak
A heretic amongst you … don't you let me live too long

Burn!

Could you imagine the pain
Why would my countrymen let me down
They're bearing witness just to save their skin
That this might keep them from burning
They'd sell their mothers just to save their skin
That this might keep them alive

The marks I'm bearing are oh so deep
My will ingrained at birth
To flood true darkness with light and reverse
You'll see my covenant to keep

Your judgment in the hands of the most inept
Condemn those similar to burn with me
But the night is still young … I'm also feeling very bold
I think I'll do some burning of my own

This is a song about a betrayal that I had experienced—not from any one person but from a number of things that were happening at the time. I wasn't complaining about it, though—I was reveling in it, and asking questions about pure betrayal: *Are you going to come and burn with me? You threw me in this fire, come and join me.*

The image of the horses foaming, as they do when you ride them hard, creates a visual subset to underline the effort that goes into things. If someone is just traveling along and getting after something, it takes the severity of the impending doom away if it's lackadaisical, so I make sure to use as many descriptors as possible to enhance the urgency of whatever it is. I'll take positive and/or negative experiences and use them as I wish to tell a story.

I realize that the song seems to end on a threat, but I was chuckling to myself as I wrote that last line. It's almost like taking the perspective of the movie *Apocalypse Now*, and how Lieutenant Colonel Bill Kilgore is walking along the beach, saying, 'I love the smell of napalm in the morning.' Sometimes it can be therapeutic to write these songs. It entertains me a lot, so when people hear it and like it themselves, they should know that it was written because I like it, too. A lot of times I'll say things in a way that is sarcastic and dismissive and funny about something, as if Monty Python were super-impolite, because they do a lot of parodies that poke fun at something that is lackluster or just stupid. Imagine if they did some strange skit about mixer valves, know what I mean?

Oftentimes I'll be sarcastic about something that is annoying to me, and turn it into something that at least gives me some entertainment value, as opposed to just being pissed off. It's still very easy for me to write angry songs, even though I'm much less angry these days. I've become a great deal better at compartmentalizing things.

HATEWORK

FROM *DOMINATION*, 1995

Hatework
Bringer of doom
Hatework

What I have in store
What has the devil got to do with it
I'm brewing my toil
So the brimstone comes this way

Nightwork
My life's work
Nightwork … world in flames

This calls for fire
This is a call for ruin
We will be departed
Leave the rot so lonely

Hatework
Bringer of doom
Hatework … and the turmoil comes
Hatework
My work
Hatework … and the earth's left burning

I call death … death is answering me
And a world betrayed is black forever

I wrote this song in about five minutes, completely off the cuff. Erik Rutan composed the music and spent a lot of time orchestrating it in the studio. I think it's brilliant. When I heard it, I was so blown away and inspired. It turned into this grueling, anthemic dirge, if you will. We always had at least one track on many of these records that was way out in left field, and I think in the case of *Domination*, it was this song, because it was completely different to everything else. It was still very powerful and majestic, though.

The lyrics were written on the spur of the moment: I was thinking like a witch or a warlock with a cauldron, and putting all this wicked emotion into it, and not attributing it to anything other than just fury. It's all dark imagery that becomes poetry.

· chapter eight ·

THE ULTIMATUM

"Maximize your potential, stay healthy, be prepared—and give some thought to the future of society."

I stopped worrying a long time ago about what everybody else thinks about what I do. We're not in junior high anymore, and everybody needs to take ownership and responsibility for themselves. My objective is to concentrate on myself and the things that I need to do. I can't be considering things that shouldn't need to be considered.

This attitude has left me free to explore a whole range of creative options since I parted ways with Morbid Angel.

At this point in my life, even more so than ever, it's really just about honesty in music. For me, it's about doing what you feel. Sometimes folks will like one thing and not like another, and so on, but the most important thing to me is being true to myself and being who I am. I've had haters my whole life, so I'm not really concerned about those things—I can't be.

I'm a metal guy, and I always will be; that's how I cut my teeth, and it's really where I'm at, but there are other things that I've found that are fun and enjoyable. They give me a chance to cross paths and rub elbows with other musicians that are not metal people, but who are insanely good players nonetheless. A lot of it is a journey for me: *Let's go over here. Do I like any of this? That's kind of cool, let's try something,* just as I always have.

One of these creative avenues is outlaw country music, although I don't play it often—it's more for special occasions. I do a few shows a year, depending on how much time I have and whether everything makes sense. We did a show on Halloween 2017, here in Austin, and there were a lot of guys there who sounded like other people; I was the only one who sounded like me. When I got there, a bunch of metal guys were standing there watching me, and when I got offstage I had a chance to visit with them.

One guy said, 'Man, I came here to see this.'

I replied, 'Okay, I hope you liked it.'

He said, 'I did, but I expected it to suck.'

'Why would you say that?' I asked.

He said, 'I don't know … you don't really have a history with this kind of music.'

'Not to your knowledge, perhaps, but I grew up listening to a lot of this stuff,' I told him.

This is representative of a lot of people's views about me playing country songs. It's just more music that I do. I'm trying to expand as opposed to narrow, rather than do one single thing and go in any one direction. I keep everything real separate, but it's all coming from the same place. I wouldn't want to do a show, for example, where I mixed the sets—playing a Morbid track and a country track. I'm capable of doing it, but the emotions are coming from a different place.

I did a couple of cool videos, too. This came about when Randy Blythe of Lamb Of God and I were at one of Phil Anselmo's horror attractions, and a couple of film guys were there. One of them asked me if I'd mind doing a cameo in a low-budget horror movie he was making called *Hair Metal Zombie Massacre*. Randy and I made a brief cameo where we're heckling a band. It's a quick one-take scene, which we did on the spot.

I ended up becoming friends with this guy, Josh Vargas, and he said, 'Man, if you ever need any music videos directing, let me know, and I'll do you a solid,' and I said, 'I might just take you up on that.' When I did my country single, 'Drinkin' With The Devil,' I wanted to do a video for it, and I called Josh. He said, 'I'd fuckin' love to do that!' because it took him out of his element a bit, but it was cool enough so that he totally got it. A lot of these Texas guys have musical interests that go in all different directions.

I'm really pleased with the way the video turned out. It's the exact flavor that I was looking for. A little cheeky, but still to the point. It wasn't modern, it had a timeless feel—rootsy and really fun.

Another project came along called Headcat, which was a vehicle for the rockabilly interests of the late Ian 'Lemmy' Kilmister of Motörhead. Danny Harvey, who plays guitar in my country band, also plays in Headcat, which came about when the Wacken Festival in Germany did a special tribute to Lemmy.

When the guys asked me if I'd be interested in recording a few songs and playing a few shows with Headcat, I was like, 'Okay, although I don't really sound like Lemmy'—but it worked, in its own way. I had a lot of fun doing it, because it was so different from anything I'd done before. I wouldn't say it's really a challenge from a playing standpoint, but feeling it and getting after it was a lot of fun; I enjoy it quite a bit.

It's basically loud, roots-based rock'n'roll from the fifties and sixties that is turned up a little louder than it should be. It's intuitive, too; when we added a particular song to the set, I remember saying, 'I don't know this song, I've never heard it before,' and Danny said, 'Yes you do; it's in A, just follow my lead.' I did, and we got through the song, and he said, 'I told you you knew it!' I'm not used to that, because extreme metal is very deliberate, not jammed. There's not a lot of room to walk the bass around it.

Wacken was amazing, as always. Some of these summer festivals in Europe are just great—it's not like the Ozzfest, where they play the same show in every city. A festival is an event, and I wish we had something similar in the States—a three-day festival with a whole bunch of really diverse bands, not just one kind of music.

If you don't show up, you miss it—again, it's not like the Ozzfest, where you can just say, *I'll wait till it comes to my town.* It encourages fan involvement, and if you're really a fan you'll jump on a plane and plan your summer vacation around a few festivals. That way you'll see bands playing together who would never share a stage on a small tour. I've always thought that was really cool, and hats off to those guys for still making that special.

I treasure the songs I wrote in Morbid Angel, so after my country songs and Headcat came to fruition, I formed a new band, I Am Morbid, in which we play the Morbid songs that I wrote. We announced it toward the end of 2016, and we toured the following year. I rehearsed the Headcat and I Am Morbid projects one right after the other.

The tour was great and the venues were packed, but the aim with I Am Morbid is to play festival dates rather than set up a tour grind where we get on a bus and be gone for months at a time. There's no reason for that, and none of us are particularly interested in doing it, because I've been doing that since I was a teenager, and you get to a point where you don't want to do it any more. I love performing, and people are happy to see these performances, and it's a part of the portfolio, so there's no reason not to do it.

There was some commentary from the Morbid Angel camp, but for a lot of these things no response from me is necessary. That says it all. I didn't have to respond because everyone else did on my behalf. Who's going to sing my songs—a replacement? I'm very passionate about my work, and, as has been said, I'm not very good at being other people, but I'm real good at being me.

Of course, Tim Yeung and I have been working together for many years now, and the two guitar players, who are friends of mine, are both well-established, with lots of history and credibility, but it's different. They can play it, but their feel is a little more like a band, and it feels really good to be onstage when we play.

It feels like everybody is performing, and the way that it gels is considerably different to the way it was in the past. It's nice when band-members are friends, but someone being my best friend is not necessarily a precursor to being in a band together. If we can get along for a couple of hours onstage and the music feels good, it starts there. I genuinely like these guys, though, and you start realizing that life is too short to have people in your life that are detractors. It's not worth it.

All this reminds me of how I used to be a much more intolerant person when I was younger. I feel like I've really put a lot of that aside, because in many ways it led to a lot of negativity. That's wasted energy at this point. It's much easier to dismiss something that doesn't work and move on to something that does.

In 2018, I teamed up with Rune Eriksen, who was the guitarist in the band Mayhem for many years, and Flo Mounier of Cryptopsy, a phenomenal drummer. Our new band, Vltimas (pronounced Ultimas) released a debut album, *Something Wicked Marches In*, in March 2019, when I was working on this book.

I've been friends with and a fan of Rune for a number of years. In my mind, he almost singlehandedly defined a particular guitar style as it relates to what we would consider Norwegian black metal.

We had hung out a bit over the years, and he called me out of the blue, asked what I was up to, and suggested that we should get together one day and make some music. I replied, 'Why is that day not today?' and he told me that was the answer he was hoping for. He already had this idea put together with Season Of Mist; he and Flo had already started working on some music. The guys came out; we met three times and started putting some music together.

The Vltimas songs weren't complete when I came along. In most cases, Rune had between one and three riffs that worked well off of each other. All the structure was done with the three of us sitting in a room. We gave the songs working titles. We'd call them something just so we know what songs we're referring to, and it was usually something silly or obscene. Later, we'd commit them to memory under their real titles.

There was one thing that worked particularly well on that album. We had two songs that had a certain feel: one was marching in and one was marching out, and although those two ended up getting reversed, I went with that theme because it seemed really fitting, and I ended up with 'Something Wicked Marches In' and 'Marching On,' the last song on the record. Those two songs had working titles that ended up as part of their final titles. They spoke to the introduction of this new monster that we had created, but that was as yet undefined, because it will define itself over a multi-year, multi-album quest.

Let me be clear about this record: I think it's breathtakingly good. It's well beyond anything I've ever done. I don't even know what to call it. I listen to it and it doesn't sound like anything I know. Our producer, Jaime Gomez Arellano, is originally from Colombia, but he lives in Woburn, in England, where we recorded the album. He did Ghost's first record, and he did a number of things with Paradise Lost and Sunn O))), and he's really into analogue equipment. The only thing that's sampled on the album is the kick drum, which you pretty much need to do with anything that's fast. Everything else is natural, with actual guitar amps.

The music pulled everyone out of their comfort zone a little, because there's a lot of stuff that's very melodic and orchestrated. When I listen to it, I hear Wagner, because we pulled out the stops and didn't say no to anything. I'm using many of the weapons in my vocal arsenal, and we'll keep pushing the envelope as far as we can.

Obviously, everybody has busy schedules, and we all live in different places, which is somewhat of a hindrance. It would be easy if everyone lived two doors down from one another, as opposed to in multiple countries, but we managed to make it work—and we're virtually ready to record another album.

The music is the most lush, misanthropic soundtrack you've ever heard. It's really clear, so there's no mistaking what I say, with or without a lyric sheet. It's loud and proud, and there's nothing bashful.

I'm proud of the whole damn record, but purely from the live performance standpoint, I particularly like 'Last Ones Alive Win Nothing.' I can see the audience is really into it, because it has such a deep groove, and the story is one hundred percent true. Not everybody knows it yet, but time will show that it's true. It feels great to perform it, and I can tell that it really makes a connection with the audience as well.

There was a film, *The Omega Man*, which came out in 1971, and which starred Charlton Heston. In some respects, it was part of the inspiration for 'Last Ones Alive Win Nothing.' It's a statement about the human condition, and the lack of historical reference that folks put in their day-to-day life. When we die we take nothing with us, other than our legacy. Everyone's in a race to accumulate all this stuff, and then you die and you've won nothing. Nothing ventured, nothing gained: it's almost celebrating that knowledge. It's not negative—when you revel in truth it's a positive, even if the truth is not necessarily to our liking. We have to be comfortable with what is, at the end of the day.

With the release date of the Vltimas record being at the end of March, all of the summer festivals were already booked, as they usually are, a year in advance. It was only by the good graces of Michael Berberian at Season Of Mist that we played Wacken in the summer of 2019. He set up a private stream and sent it to a couple of promoters, saying, 'Hey listen, we're really behind this, we know it's late in the game but if you can find a spot, we'd really like Vltimas to play.'

We set up a week of rehearsals in Holland and played two club shows just to get our feet wet, then went on to do Hellfest and Mystic Fest and Tons Of Rock. At the eleventh hour, Copenhell came along, too, and that ended up being our first show. Because of the success of those shows in the press, we did three more festivals. It was awesome. People are starved for content these days, and I'm happy to give it to them.

> ***"Take opportunities as they come to you. Be courageous, and keep your eyes and mind open, because you never know what gifts will be handed to you, or when."***

EXISTO VULGORÉ

FROM *ILLUD DIVINUM INSANUS*, 2011

My sour images dispelling all doubt
One sip of poison and my darkness comes out
Like glass reflecting all the venom I see
My spirit taken task and now I will forever be

Vulgore of the gory
Vulgore for the glory glory
Vulgore tells the ugly story
Vulgore existo vulgoré

All the worldly deeds of malice displayed
From a wicked recipe this potion is made
Each drop of future's bleak and callused in view
Sick clerics unprepared for vulgore I spew

I rejoice in awful ways
I sickly tune the worst of days
To have unreason's show to tell
All the world is a victim 'cause I'm raising hell

Go gore the race is on to find a pure one
With simple subjects
Oh this never could be fun
Gore spreads a santo duelo como nino
Feliz un día cuando gore golpea

Vulgore is a made-up word—it had a ring to it. It is 'vulgar,' yes, but I created this character, and his name is Vulgore. He's the gothic Mr. Hyde, if you will.

I looked on my character in the video for this song as a kind of Jekyll and Hyde person, and I make references to that in the song—about being an individual, and my darkness coming out. I look at him as being an alter ego who takes a dose of his potion and becomes the embodiment of the ugliness that he dislikes.

I don't know that everybody has that same darkness in them. I don't know that people necessarily take the time out to really study the guy in the mirror. There are probably different degrees of awareness that any individual may have. I've gone out of my way to really know myself, because at the end of the day I need to be my own best friend. It starts there, and everything that I do is an extension of that.

TOO EXTREME!

FROM *ILLUD DIVINUM INSANUS*, 2011

Panic
This is your one warning
Pounding, pounding ... you feel it
Burning, burning this lava
Scorching weakened hearts be troubled
They scream we're too extreme

We come to spread our insane
This doctrine chaos chaos
Demanding nothing less but to
Make you scream we're too extreme

Tu corazón latiendo
Te sientes el dolor
Deseo la locura
Tu gritas … Extreme!

Welcome to your new religion
We come collecting souls
You come to sing our praises
Together selfless

We are your new religion
No religion
Extreme!

De sud America
A puertas de oro athens
A la quema inframundo
Conmigo … Extreme

Visión sufrirá
Orejas derretirá
Bese su nueva creencia
Es nombre Extreme

We are your new religion
No religion

You come to us in torment
And we make your bodies heave
Our sounds invoke your demon
Together too extreme!

This track was completely out of left field in many ways, so all I could think of was making it worse, and being as animalistic as possible. It's really a very strange track. A lot of people really didn't care for it, and I get that, but when you're in a band situation, you work toward a goal.

Could we have removed a lot of that stuff and made it sound more like a traditional track that sounded like it came from *Covenant* or *Domination*? Probably, but that's not where Trey was. He came in and he'd make something that was kind of a demo of what he was after, and then it was up to us to figure out what it was and what was going on. I thought, *This is weird and over the top, so let's make it more so.*

A song can start with a phrase, or a couple of sentences that work well together and move through a theme pretty quickly, or it can start with a melody, or just a couple of chords. It can be a song that someone presents me with, or just a couple of riffs that someone gives me. I open myself to it and let the music move me in a direction that I feel is appropriate. There's not really one way to do anything, and I like all the different ways, because each one is a new frontier and a new challenge.

The Spanish lyrics are a tribute to the fans of Morbid Angel in Central and South America. I have a little bit of Spanish, and, when

I'm immersed in it, it gets better out of necessity. Our producer/engineer, Punchy, has a Cuban background, so he had his father, who is a theater guy, take a look at it to see if it made sense. He said, 'It's a very strange way of saying what you're trying to say, but it's artistic. It's not improper,' and he got a kick out of it. He asked, 'Where does this come from?' and I said, 'I don't know, but I want language and utterances not to be a barrier, and I like to get myself out of my safe zone.' I take a lot of liberties with language, including the English language. The song's so damn unsafe to begin with that I wanted to pour some gas on the fire.

I AM MORBID

FROM *ILLUD DIVINUM INSANUS*, 2011

We stand defiant
In this great big ugly world
Do believe that the chaos
Was our one true calling
First we muscled fate
Then we brazenly call disorder
Watch the normals cower
They just can't take it anymore

Withstand together now
All the damning from on high
Fist horns are roaring forth
As I scream into the sky

I'm morbid
Morbid and
Sordid
Distorted
Bring them to their knees
I'm morbid
Morbid
Won't be thwarted
From celebrating morbid victories

We're seen as monsters, merely being
Is a threat to all
What can't destroy us makes us strong
And in a twisted mind
Oh everything is possible
And in a twist of fate
We make it all come down … Crumbling down
Oh we'll bring them down

We stand invincible not just a dream
Straight from the underground we scream

I'm morbid

We stand invincible not just a dream
Straight from the underground
The gods are screaming

Tear down the obstacles this is our way
We're born to quake the world
There is no other way

I'm morbid

There is a deeper meaning to 'morbid' than simply being obsessed with death: there always has been. There are other ways of defining it within ourselves, but I've taken it to mean that the obsession with all things dark gives you the strength to move forward. It's casting aside conventional Judeo-Christian beliefs in a higher power and putting it squarely on the strength of the individual will.

'We' in the song are myself and my kindred folk: those who choose to walk the Left-Hand Path, those who choose to educate themselves, those who dig deeper into things, those who don't accept something just because there's a horde of people who accept it.

We are people who look beyond: we scratch beneath the surface, we test the authenticity of things. We are those who look in the mirror and have very critical conversations with the person staring back at them—and we use that critical relationship as a pillar of strength, rather than something that is suggested to them by man, god, or government. It's all very simple. It sounds complex, but at the end of the day, once the compass is correct, everything automatically goes through this type of thought process. It's really not difficult: it's a normal, natural thing to me. At any given point, I can decide, *How far do I take this? Is it a battle, or something that I just simply remain silent on and allow something to be whatever it's going to be if I don't personally have a vested interest in it?*

• chapter nine •

RELEASE THIS FURY

"Songwriting is, to me, about using the wisdom that life teaches us, and therefore, as a songwriter, I welcome those teachings. What can we learn from bending our will toward the creation of a song?"

Songwriting is a craft, and there are several different ways in which I go about it, depending on whether I'm working on my own or with others. The only rule is the one of integrity. I don't have a preference, because different things take on different shapes.

I probably write songs every day, whether I know it or not. I wake up in the morning and sing songs to the cat, or, if I'm disgusted about something, I may write something in the elevator on the way up to whatever floor I'm going to, just to marginalize the aggravation of a given subject or situation. Or, if I'm standing in line, waiting for something, I'll create little parodies or jingles, just to express some emotion. It's a way to turn something negative into something funny.

Is everything in life an inspiration for songwriting? Unfortunately, yes! Every day, some event takes place that inspires me to write a few lines. It doesn't matter where I am or what I'm doing—something happens that I use for some form of inspiration. Whether I take it to the next step or not and make a full song out of it is purely incidental.

Thinking about how I write lyrics, the acquisition of knowledge has become more important to me as time goes by. It's a gift, if you will. Not everyone would agree with that terminology, but that's the way it's intended. I don't remember ever hearing someone say, 'I wish I had less knowledge.'

We used to amuse ourselves in Morbid Angel about that very phrase. Like a mechanic saying, 'Gosh, I wish I didn't have as many tools as I do,' or someone looking at a menu in a restaurant and saying, 'I wish there weren't so many choices.' The more there is, the more we can grow. There's always been a quest for knowledge, and more knowledge.

Now, sometimes it can become overwhelming. The internet has certainly opened up the possibility of literally being on overload every day; there are things coming at us constantly from left, right, and center, above and below. That can be too much at times. I personally get overwhelmed when I'm sitting on an airplane, traveling overseas, and the seat back screen wants to market to me. I cover it up, because if someone's going to market to me then they're going to pay me.

I remember a flight attendant coming by one time and saying, 'Sir, you need to uncover this,' and I replied, 'Not unless I'm on the clock.' She didn't understand, so I took ten seconds to explain it to her, and she said, 'Okay.' It's hard to get out of bed in the morning without the marketing of this, that, or the other taking place. There are times when simplicity appeals to me, just to refresh myself for the next battle.

Another important step is to try to stay current. There are some things that I want to at least have the knowledge of, although whether they become part of my choices or my being is a different story. These go through the same filter that anything would. I remember my grandparents and others who were much older than me saying, 'Oh, kids these days,' and similar things. My parents said these things, too. I don't want to become that person myself.

In some ways, we're programmed to think that way after a certain age, but when I think about it, there were generations before us that did great things. They ran down a path that, historically speaking, was very destructive and very damaging. Now, there's also the argument that you have to tear something down in order to rebuild it, but if something looks, smells, and tastes like something that history would indicate is not a good idea, as if we've been here before, and we've tried this before and it doesn't work, then that filter is pretty strong in my life.

Sometimes these things are a passing phase, and I look back and I think about all the people who were propagating something—whether it be music, or a lifestyle, or some social belief—and it ends up going by the wayside, then I think to myself, *Well, that's pretty much how I felt about it when I first learned of it.* I don't think that I'm any different from anyone else who has been on the planet for a while, and who has basically decided what their likes and dislikes are. Still, I really make every attempt to keep an open mind on things that might be new. If it's not new and it's a resurrection of something from the past that has failed, then my filter catches it.

Do I think people are capable of having their minds expanded by music? Yes, but this is where it gets complicated. To an extent, live and let live, or live and let die—whichever you prefer—is nice, when there's not a lot of entanglement. I'll do what I do, and that's not going to change. I'm not going to be pompous enough to think that somehow I need to impose my beliefs on anyone else.

Thankfully, it's a big planet, and there are areas where people can do whatever it is that they want to do—I don't want to stop them, but they should do it wherever they are, and likewise not impose it on me. Because if I have to get involved, then there's another battle.

There's one thing that I always try to plan for—the ability to not plan. I've always felt that spontaneity in life, and leaving room for chaos, and spur-of-the-moment actions without thought, leads to some unpredictable outcomes. As an artist, I always want to leave room for those kinds of things. If everything is so thought-out and planned all the time, it feels stale to me. A lot of times, I want to show up, and I want a given studio session to have an atmosphere and the circumstances surrounding it to be a factor in the outcome.

I can plan all I want, and I do that, but there's something that is so quick and honest and organic in spontaneity. There are other times when I don't want to commit to ideas until I've opened myself up to the influences of the aura around me. The aura could be the setting, whether that's a studio or out in seclusion in the mountains somewhere, or it could be under intense pressure, or it could be during or after a night of unreasonable libation.

All of these things apply—I don't want to have one single way where it starts to feel like you're working in a fast-food restaurant, with a burger prepared exactly the same way every time. That's totally boring, and it would make me not want to do anything, so I always like to have some new stimulus.

For example, with the Vltimas record, I had three tracks basically complete, and ideas for others, but some I didn't want to have any idea of at all until I got in the studio. I had themes, I had titles, and I knew essentially the type of direction that I was going to go in, but I didn't want to put pen to paper until it was literally, *You're on. Go!* Sometimes that pressure helps.

I'm always prepared with my skillset, but I don't always want to be so prepared with exactly what it is that I'm going to do, because sometimes I surprise myself. There is a kick that I get out of composing spontaneously, although I'm not as good at it as some people are. They're so good at it that I'm jealous.

Paul McCartney is a prime example: I saw him on TV in front of a live audience, saying, 'Let's write a song.' He had everything miked up, so he made a few loops on drums and played some guitar and bass, and then started singing over the top of it. It didn't seem that he had planned any of it, and it was so good that I was thinking, *All he has to do is those few things and he's got the next Abbey Road album.*

Some people are much better at it, or they employ a different skillset, and in his case he's just so good and gifted. We all have our cross to bear. He does it his way, I do it my way. I always look up to people who have that level of chutzpah to get out there and do it. In his case, it all came out so organic that it was humbling, because he was humble as he was doing it. And if there's anyone who deserves not to have to be humble at all, it's someone who has achieved as much as he has.

There are also different ways to go about fitting the rhythms of the lyrics to the music. Sometimes those ways are obvious, where everything is patterned directly with the drums. I do a little bit of that, although I generally find it boring. I like to play off the beat, doing things that stretch it and make it a little bit more expressive, because it's really all about expressing personality at the end of the day.

I have a pretty big personality, so I like to move things around and dance with words and get phrasing that, to me, bounces off the music a little bit. Most other forms of music do that, and I don't see any reason why it shouldn't happen in extreme metal. Of course, some people just don't feel it, because everyone is different. Understandably, a lot of writers are different to me, based on what I do and what others do. I'm pretty good at being me; I'm not very good at being anyone else.

⛤

While we're talking about making music, here's a quick word on my musical equipment, for those who are interested.

I started on upright bass in the school orchestra in fifth grade, but, like I said earlier, I didn't really take it seriously: there was a girl I liked in the orchestra, which is why I was there. It definitely helped my left-hand technique a little, though. I was taught the formal way to play, and from there I found a natural, comfortable way to do it. I still like upright bass quite a bit, and I have a couple of them, which I mess with from time to time.

I moved to bass guitar when I was about fifteen. I have a really low voice, and I hear low frequencies. I would play air bass when I was a kid, listening to records, and it seemed really natural for me. The music that inspired me always had really prominent bass: guys like Geezer Butler, Mel Schacher from Grand Funk Railroad, Dennis Dunaway from Alice Cooper's band, and later Gene Simmons, although it took me a while to appreciate KISS. I worked at it, and I've got a good ear, so I picked stuff up quickly, and I practiced techniques while listening to different players.

I picked up a lot of stuff for the right hand from Steve Harris of Iron Maiden. I literally sat down and listened to Iron Maiden songs and practiced galloping with my right hand. I'd go and see bands and see bassists using a pick, and I'd be all, *Oh, he uses a pick* … and I'd get on my high horse about it. But then I saw Accept and saw how synchronized their bassist, Peter Baltes, was with the double kick drums, keeping everything really tight, which caused me to pause and think how that works from a musical standpoint. It then became apparent that both styles are important.

I studied a little bit of theory, but the problem is that it makes me think. I don't want to think, I want to feel! I can follow it, slowly, but it doesn't seem musical to me. There are a lot of really great players who say that you've got to read sheet music because it helps you make a certain amount of money per hour in the studio, but that's not what I'm into music for: I'm into music for the feeling. Theory is important—it's just not important for me.

You can see me playing a Takamine bass in early live clips. I bought it because the shape was really cool: I saw it in a music store and I scooped it up immediately. It was pretty metal … I enjoyed playing it, but it's not where I am now; I haven't played it in quite some time. It wasn't a recording bass. I had a couple of Hamers, which I was really big on for several years.

I've had a lot of cool instruments, and each one has had its own place and time. In the very early days, I had a Washburn; an Alembic with an Explorer shape, like an Entwistle model; a Kramer, with an aluminum neck; and a Gibson EB2. You can make any bass sound good—it's all how you play it. If you own it, it's good.

I had a BC Rich Ironbird for fifteen minutes. I liked the way it looked, so I brought it home, strapped it on, and it did a nosedive: it was super neck-heavy, and that was intolerable, so I packed it up and took it back to the store. I think BC Rich basses are a work of art, it's just that their balance is not comfortable on the body. The shapes are very artistic; in fact, they always have been. I'll give a bit for a bass that I like, but I'm not gonna give that much. It's a labor of love: farmers have to cultivate their fields, and players have to cultivate their instruments.

My main pedal for some time has been a Jim Dunlop MXR

M80, which is the nicest, most usable effect I've found in years. I love the way you can keep the low end when you punch in the distortion, and the mids are nice and gritty. For amps, I've been an Ampeg SVT user for a long time—since the early eighties—and recently I've gotten together with a company from Brazil called Meteoro. They make amps that are very familiar to me in the way they operate, but they have a lot of power.

My go-to bass now is my signature Dean Demonator. When I was visiting one day, Elliott Rubinson, the owner of Dean, asked me if there were any Dean guitars I liked. I said that I had a lot of instruments, and that there was nothing that really met my needs there. He said, 'I'm not going to settle for that. Let's get together with our luthier and come up with something that you do like.' It was game on, so we spent three months going back and forth to find the right design, and to this day I'm really, really happy with it.

I love the way the Demonator plays and sounds, and how it sits when you play it. It has an interesting shape that isn't seen anywhere else, and it's totally metal. There were two new models a while back: one which is a set neck rather than a neck-through, and then a limited run of US-made Demonators that are really gorgeous, with a brass pentagram inset into them. That is a marvelous instrument. I don't want to take them out of the house.

I don't play five-strings. I like a narrow nut, and I like to play my basses really low, and I would have to raise it higher than I'd like to. We tuned the guitars in Morbid Angel to A# for several songs, so I added a low B-string to my bass and dropped the high G. I'll play triads or quads with three fingers. It's really percussive: the way I practiced it was to mute the strings and make sure that the pressure

I applied to the strings was as even as humanly possible. One finger wasn't quieter than the other.

Being a musician is down to being all about music from the moment you wake up, and having it flowing through your veins. You do your rehearsals and your listening, and you're all about it. Music is not something you can turn on and off. That's important to me.

Another thing that has always been important to me is being articulate with my vocals. The only other singer in our genre of metal I knew who went that way was Chuck Schuldiner. He sang very clearly, too, even within the guttural style.

There's so much music that I hear today where the vocals sound like a lawnmower. It makes me wonder if the songwriters don't have anything to say, or if it's not important to them that it's understandable. And don't get me started on band logos that you can't read, which are ludicrous; after all, a business with a sign that you can't read is a sign of poor business. It's ridiculous that bands want the most unreadable logo possible.

And then there's the live aspect. With any of these projects, I don't headbang as much as I used to, because of neck injuries that I've sustained, but I don't think I'm alone in that. I feel the music and I want to move my body, but headbanging to the degree that I did it when I was in my twenties is off the table. You go through life and things start to hurt more—but I feel the music, and there will always be the level of passion in my performances that there ever has been.

The music industry is a mess. It's never been a particularly glamorous industry to inhabit anyway, even though appearances may make it look as if it is. It continues to evolve and do whatever it's going to do, and fortunately there's some really good music out there, as well as some really lousy stuff. That's always been the way, but there are a lot more people putting music out nowadays; it used to be a lot more expensive to make music and release it. There's a lot more music to choose from, but a lot of shit as well, as the law of averages tells us.

I've also had a couple of film roles in recent years. The first of these was a voiceover part in *Realm Of The Damned*, a horror movie based on still images from a graphic novel. The challenge for me was adding character to an unanimated character. The way that it was shot, using still photos, meant that emotionally attaching yourself was challenging. But we had a good director, and I'm pleased with the outcome.

Golgotha is a live-action film in which I play a priest who is trying to counsel people at the same time as battling his own demons. He ends up committing suicide on film—if I were a priest in real life, I would probably want to commit suicide, too.

Acting, for me, is about adding emotion to the character so it's portrayed the way the director wants; good direction is key. When we went in, I had a bunch of questions about how old the priest was, where he was from, and what experiences he'd had, because I needed to know who this guy is, as he's not me. I need this data so I can formulate how he would feel if a given thing happened. Performing has never been a problem for me, but for me to do it to someone else's vision, I need a good director.

At this point, between the country music, the two metal bands, and playing rock'n'roll with Headcat, I'm pretty well satisfied. The number of things I get asked to do is endless, and most of the time I politely decline. I ask myself how I feel about it, and I have to like either the music or the person in order to do it.

But who knows? If it involves being creative with music or film, I'm generally interested in doing it. For example, on our 2019 European tour dates, Vltimas played a version of 'Black Sabbath.' We just wanted to do something that was an ode to one of the most important bands that led the genre that we know of as metal—any kind of metal, whether heavy or extreme metal. Tony Iommi and Geezer Butler can easily take credit where it's due, and to my mind they should, because there wouldn't be this kind of music without Black Sabbath.

The Vltimas record is short and to the point, so, just as if *Reign In Blood* had been Slayer's first record and they'd gone out and played that record in its entirety, playing 'Black Sabbath,' as well as being what we felt was a fitting tribute, was a good way to extend the set. Rune suggested it, and I thought it was a great choice.

You have to own everything you do, otherwise it's just a cover, so we enhanced it by making the song as personal as possible. Not so different from other people who have done brilliant remakes of stuff. At the risk of sounding profane, I think Disturbed's version of 'The Sound Of Silence' is better than the original.

Of course, I've evolved as a songwriter. As we grow as people, things change, and skillsets become more honed and more refined. I don't know whether we always try to improve, or whether it's a natural evolution that comes with time spent on the planet.

For me, a song could start with me sitting on a sofa with an acoustic guitar. Oftentimes I'll hear it in my head before we actually start recording something or writing it down. I might hear a vocal melody or a chord sequence. These days it usually starts with a chorus, which I write when a theme for the song comes to mind, and then I'll fill in the details around that. If I'm working with other songwriters, maybe I'll hear a certain riff and attach something to that in my mind. Then I'll come up with a theme and take a piece of music, which is the way I worked with Rune on Vltimas.

With him, I listen to a riff that moves me in a certain way, and often, straight out of the gate, I'll hear it and know exactly where I'm going with it. It's not even a challenge. I'll work up a good portion of it and then go back in with the arrangement and say, 'This is absolutely the chorus, here's some verses,' and think about it as a theme. The chorus always takes it right back home and puts it in the spotlight, and the details are the salt and pepper and all the ingredients that it takes to get to the grand dish.

In essence, I look at a song as a story, often with a beginning, a progression, and an end, and with a theme, although there doesn't have to be an ending. There will be a 'to be continued,' until I write my swansong in a hospital bed somewhere. I redraft my lyrics, too, in order to make them as complete as I can. Sometimes I'll write a song and it is recorded exactly as it is; other times I'll get into a trap with bouncy phrasing and not being straight with the beat, or there will be more words than I can comfortably enunciate, because I don't leave room for a breath, so I'll go back and remove a few. With modern studio trickery you can get around that, but then you're in trouble if you ever do the song live. You're writing yourself a check that you can't cash.

There are vowels and consonants that are more difficult to

sing than others, or which require a particular mouth movement to achieve. None of this is easy to do, but because I want to be clear and articulate, I try to avoid setting myself traps. I rehearse in my mind the kind of performance and delivery I want to do, which can be chanting gibberish over a riff, just to establish how the pattern feels as it comes out. I make shapes with my palate and then turn them into words, knowing where I want the words to be and how I want them to feel. A song can start right there, just with phonetic shapes that tell me where I want to come in, where I want to lay back a little bit and where I want to hit it real hard. It's really more about feeling than anything else. Everything coalesces together in the end.

On that subject, song arrangements are my biggest thing, because when things flow and come together the way they should, I'm happy. I might suggest two more rounds on a riff before we change, for example, just to let the vocals flow. I may be hearing things in other people's music that they wouldn't, and so we negotiate it with explanations as to why it would be a good idea. You have creative trust with people, and everyone has their area, but at the same time we might suggest a different drum fill or chord and so on.

Generally speaking, once the lyrics are in my memory, they're in there permanently. I might depart from the lyrics from a performance perspective and do something different from the recorded song, because I enjoy it when a band plays a song a little differently from the album. If it's going to sound exactly like the CD, then why not buy the CD, because it'll sound better?

Some artists completely rearrange stuff, or add additional

choruses or jam parts to songs, and I personally appreciate that, because it's another rendition of something that I already liked. I learned how to do this from the order of the set, which is designed to be a rollercoaster ride—for me, anyway.

Do I think that the same audience is listening these days? Well, I mentioned the film *Caligula* earlier. Films like that would never be made today. They're not immediate enough, and there wouldn't be enough interest. Here I am sounding like an old person, but there's evidence to show that a lot of culture has been lost because it's not immediate enough for the short attention span of these days, which is too bad, because I like what I like, and many of my comrades are also into those things, but the general public doesn't seem to have much appetite for things that are not so immediate anymore.

It's true of music, too. Listen to the way that songs are written nowadays versus in the seventies, and which instruments occupy which place, and how the studio sessions came out. Listen to the type of playing that was happening on the old Black Sabbath and Grand Funk Railroad and Yes albums. People actually got in there and played: it wasn't just start-stop, overdub, and Pro Tools it to death until it sounds right—people bared their souls and became a unit in the studio. They may have thrown a few vocals and solos over the top of it but, by and large, it was live, and you can hear that it's live.

It appears that the world is moving toward formula and away from spontaneity. I don't revel in it but it seems that way. The days of huge opera houses being as grandiose as they were a hundred years ago are gone; the populace just doesn't care about these things the way they used to.

Sometimes, quality still filters to the surface, but you have a formula, and you know it's going to be designed more to appeal to a short attention span. When that's done, the machine spits out something else that's similar, because there are metrics about what people listen to. It's almost like a continuous poll, to see what's going to do well, and it looks at profit first and creativity second. In my mind it should be the other way around.

Can it be reversed? One can only hope. I don't know. It seems like technology is charging along this path and leaving none left standing. Now, I don't govern my life that way, but I'm the odd man out. Does that make me wrong, or does it just make me different?

If I were king, everything would be going in a different direction, and I wouldn't make things so easy. I remember when I was a kid in first grade, building my record collection, when not everything was easy to get. It wasn't just a case of pulling up Spotify or typing in a song and it was right there—you had to go to a number of different record shops and maybe find one thing you were looking for, and then maybe hear about something else.

You'd run down these paths, because the quest was an important part of the journey. When you get too accustomed to things being so easy, and you're not putting in the work that fandom used to require, then it's not as important to you. If something comes to you quickly, it's gone just as quickly; if you work hard for something, then you have invested time and energy into a quest, and therefore the end result, generally speaking, is more important to you.

There will still be people who care enough to take the time over things as deeply as I do, but in ever-dwindling numbers. I do what I do based on my own personal compass—I'm not tooting my own trumpet here. Not everyone behaves the way that I do. But if my one legacy in life that I'm remembered for is that I helped persuade people to think a little bit more—not to tell them what to think, but to motivate them to want to dig deeper—and to be more critical about their choices, then what higher goal is there than that?

"Songwriting is, to me, the ultimate craft—the art form that elevates us beyond the merely human plane. Find your own creativity; in the end, it will save you. What's more, it will open your ears, your mind, and your life, in a world that is becoming more closed every day."

PROFUNDIS—MEA CULPA

FROM *ILLUD DIVINUM INSANUS*, 2011

Crimen profundis
I will lead the way
Divinum formidilosus impetus
I will accept all of the blame

Mea culpa … Mea mea culpa
Black will cover all and smother all
Black will never fail to bring terror for all
No traces of illumination sight without light
Under cruel reign of shadows
We will only have night
Eternal night

Illud Divinum Insane
Mea mea … Mea culpa for the terrors brought
We're the monsters, caedo caedo
And our sounds are overwrought

Grieve right live in fright fright
Grieve right live in fright fright

Illud divinum insane

Mea mea … Mea culpa
For the terrors brought

We're the monsters, caedo caedo
And our sounds are overwrought
Mea mea … Mea culpa for insanity
Twist the minds of all who hear
Our deadly sounds ever mode it be

Crimen profundis
I will lead the way
Novus lex legis profano
My sickness will lay claim

Mea culpa … Mea mea culpa
Terror's ease unease and disease
We make the mass of charlatans
Fall down to their knees
They worship but can't follow us
What stars we must be!

Majesty …

Essentially, I take responsibility for everything me, and I know how I think about things when it comes to celebrating the rebelliousness of thought. That is the message of this song.

This is not always easy. In fact, it's much more difficult at times to be the large lump that's blocking an artery, but sometimes it's necessary. I've taken shots from all different directions my whole life as a result of the philosophy and the moral compass that I govern my life by. I celebrate that.

This is a recurring theme in my life and, by extension, my music. It keeps reiterating itself, and I say it in different ways, but it's the same message and the same person, and it's all coming from the same place. 'Mea culpa' doesn't mean 'I'm sorry' here, because sorry is not a word that I use. I'll apologize from time to time, but I'm not sorry. 'Mea culpa' means 'I am responsible.'

If there's anything that I've ever tried to do, when it comes from a proselytizing standpoint, it's to get people to open their minds. Even if they close their minds to me as a result of opening their minds to other things, that's also good, because they have chosen to think critically. That's the one thing that we need so much more of from an evolutionary standpoint.

I'm not a soothsayer, but I'm inspired by them. I'm a realist, and of course we're headed down into chaos. Nature is chaos, and we do our best to make sense of all that, but I give in to it as well, and I enjoy it. Because it exists, it shouldn't be our enemy—we should find a way to make it our friend.

For this reason I used *caedo*, a Latin word that means attack, in this context. I play with Latin words because they take away from being so direct. Sometimes direct is great, and sometimes moving things around a bit is also great, because it provides for more discussion—just like you and I are having right now, dear reader.

DRINKIN' WITH THE DEVIL

SINGLE RELEASE, 2016

A man in black came out to meet me Sunday afternoon
Somehow he knew I wouldn't be at church he went straight to the saloon
I was sitting with a couple of friends as he walked in through the door
Looked right at me and told the keeper, 'Serve that man one more …
And put it on my tab.'

Well I held my breath to keep in check my curiosity
Why a stranger out of nowhere's somehow buying drinks for me
He said, 'The reason I'm here, I'll make it clear, my boss man's watching you,
So raise that glass, show some class and give the Devil his due.'

He said, 'The Devil knows you play his music and you do it well,
and he's saving your soul a special place when you finally get to hell.'
Now I've been warned about these very things for many years
But I've tended just to blow it off and tip back two more beers,
That's how I'm drinkin' with the Devil …

Drinkin' with the Devil
Tipping every bottle till they're dry
Drinkin' myself nearly six feet under
This drinkin's deviling up my smile

This fellow's talking made a few things come to mind
I listened to his take and now it's time that he heard mine

I said no disrespect to anyone but y'all just got me wrong
'Cause it ain't the Devil's handiwork that makes me write these songs

My songs are all about this crazy fucked-up world I see
Not so much about your boss man but everything 'bout me
And if playing heartfelt music friend is really such a crime
I'll sure as shit plead guilty and prepare to do my time

I'll keep on playing Devil's music and I'll do it well
And maybe I'll find that special place when I finally get to hell
Now I've been warned about these very things for many years
And still I tend to blow it off and tip back two more beers,
That's how I'm drinkin' with the Devil …

This song was written during a very intoxicated evening. It was three in the morning, out on my patio, several shots into the second bottle of tequila, and the music was just flowing.

Danny Harvey and his wife, Annie Marie Lewis, were up here to spend the night, so we were fooling around with music. Annie is a tremendous singer; I've done some stuff with her before. We actually demoed a couple of songs together that sound amazing. The timbres of our voices work really well together; there's a really authentic, old-school Southern twang to her voice that makes me melt when I hear it.

We've played a few songs together at shows, which is the way it works in Texas: you arrive at a place where someone's playing, and they're like, 'You want to get up and do a song?' 'Yes, sure, what do you want to do?' And then it happens. It's just about being in the right place at the right time, and hopefully not being too many sheets to the wind to get it done. When I'm planning to perform, of course, I make sure that libations happen after the performance, not before.

Anyway, I can bounce stuff off Annie Marie when I have a crazy idea, so I said to her, 'Follow me on this: I'm going to do one part, and here's this other part.' We were building on three- and four-part harmonies at one point, although I didn't end up recording it that way. I took walks around the neighborhood and wrote the storyline, and then sat at my computer and put up a click-track. I threw some acoustic guitars on there and sang it, and then played it for Danny. He said, 'Man, this is really fun!' so we went about getting after that and other songs.

As I mentioned elsewhere, the producer Gene 'Machine' Freeman, who had worked with Megadeth and Lamb Of God and so on, got involved after I met him at an industry conference, and he loved it because it was so out of his normal zone of activity. I wanted a nontraditional approach, and that's what he gave me. We hired a pedal-steel player, a drummer, and an upright bass player, went in to record it, and it came out exactly as I wanted it.

It didn't get attacked nearly as much as I thought it would, being that a lot of metal fans are strictly metal fans, and they don't like it when people jump out of the box. That's their problem, right?

In keeping with my thirty-five-plus-year way of life, it's a more entertaining, more fun, almost nudge-wink variant of the same damn story that I've been telling forever. In that way, it works. My goal has always been to be as honest and genuine as I can, while also throwing in some elements of grandiose entertainment and of the occult. All those things are a part of my personality.

DIABOLUS EST SANGUIS

FROM *SOMETHING WICKED MARCHES IN*, 2019

This ancient nectar boils from underground
Transforming, infects without a single sound
Bleak silent moaning as we shed our skin
Last human vestige gone and now the fun begins

Undeniable
Not regrettable
We are the cure

Blood of Devils in our veins
Blood of Devils in our veins
Blood of Devils in our veins

Confounding status quo shall be no more
All yield archaic evils long abhorred
Reveal solutions draped in mystery
A testament for martyrs destiny

Undeniable
Insurmountable
We are the cure
Blood of Devils in our veins

Demons spells
They serve us well

This noxious smell
Drive us to insanity
Recipe for total calamity

New aggressions breeding, it's a work of art
Sanguis diabolus is in our hearts
Minds set for missions of great despair
Set in motion total chaos is everywhere

Blood of Devils in our veins
Blood of Devils in our veins
Blood of Devils in our veins

This was the most, dare I say, punk-rock track that we had in Vltimas. It was noisy, and it had attitude, and when I started working on it the guys had no idea what I was going to do until I did it. I keep it that way because sometimes the element of surprise adds something. I just went in and did it, and asked, 'What do you guys think?' We made a few adjustments here and there, and one of these happened without my knowledge, so I asked, 'Hold on a minute, where's this extra part coming from? Okay, no problem, give me fifteen minutes,' and I navigated my way through it.

Sometimes we'll set little traps for each other so that we have to find a way to get in and out of it, in a musical sense. We just roared through it. It was a lot of work, especially because I was injured at the time with the snakebite to my hand, so I had some additional angst that I was dealing with while I was writing and recording. But damn, did I have fun.

• chapter ten •

GATHERED FOR A SACRED RITE

"So here we are in the twenty-first century, and what have we learned? Let's look at some important individual human issues from a rational point of view."

MONEY

It seems like the American economy is doing really well. The media is looking for reasons to be negative, but people seem to have money in their pocket. Furthermore, what people choose to do with what they've earned is not my concern. Spend it, do what you want with it. If you want to be philanthropic, that's great, but I wouldn't necessarily pass judgment or revere someone who is more philanthropic.

It's not a race to see who can be kinder, nicer, or look a certain way or whatever foolish goal people choose to pursue. If you do something, maybe do it quietly, because at the end of the day, are you doing something just to get credit for it or to be seen by others as this wonderful person? I do a lot of things that I don't really talk about.

RELIGION

There are some parts of the world where there is unrest, of course, and it would be in the world's best interest if these places settled down. Religion is still a root cause of much of this unrest, now as ever. Things are known by the effects they have on society, and I see the effects of religious beliefs every day—all you have to do is turn the news on. That belief is prevalent enough to make historical changes in the world, and has been since the dawn of time.

I have a lot of religious friends, and we just don't talk about it, because there's no point. It's all right to agree to disagree. I'm happy for anyone who has a religious belief that is helpful for them, because I want everybody to feel happy and prosper. I did what I needed to do to find the things that I needed to find, and in whatever way that manifests in somebody else's life, I'm supportive of it if it helps them find their own way to their salvation.

I'm happy. I will always be rebellious at heart, but the things that once hampered me are no longer of any consequence. I take things that used to be obstacles and turned them into advantages. I take the time to understand the basis of my beliefs and make quality observations, and reach quality conclusions, based on my own code.

I've regretted some things, and there are some things that I feel apologetic about, but I'm unapologetic about who I am. Some choices that I made hurt people who didn't deserve to be hurt, and to those people I apologize. I don't think anybody goes through life without ruffling a few feathers. I don't concentrate on that, though: it's not useful and it's not energy well spent.

A PLAUSIBLE APOCALYPSE

People should take the time to question things, and I want my music and this book to stimulate people into doing that. Sure, they may be tired after a sixty-hour workweek, and they have kids and bills to pay, and they want some downtime with a football match and a beer. The system provides us with plenty of opportunities to be distracted. A knowledgeable electorate is a dangerous electorate.

I'm an eternal optimist in many ways, but I also know that some things need to go. Some of the unsustainability of our current path is going to create a lot of pain and ugliness in the future. Even if the problem were to be addressed via heavy-handed measures, it would be really ugly, but not nearly as ugly as it's going to be when it breaks. There will be an awful lot of suffering in the future.

It's been said that the definition of lunacy is to embark on the same set of actions over and over again and expect a different result. Again, history tells us what these outcomes are going to be. Examine any event and, with a bit of rudimentary extrapolation, you'll know what's going to happen, and yet we continue to do what's expedient.

One of the biggest problems in this world is that the direction in which things are going right now is unsustainable. There's a lot of people on this planet, and there's going to be a lot more tomorrow and the day after that. We have the capacity for greatness, and it would be really nice if the striving for greatness was as important to everyone. Everybody has to find that. I can do my part by getting my show in order, and speaking to those who are close to me and maybe not so close to me, and trying to set a decent example of those kinds of things.

It is much more relaxing to peruse through a catalogue for the latest designer fashion or take in a movie or play a mindless video game than it is to be informed. The truth is that a knowledgeable citizen is a dangerous citizen. In addition, people don't want to think about these things because to do so is not comfortable. It seems that most folks are willing to eat a lot of shit rather than be confrontational, least of all with themselves.

Historically speaking, when things are unsustainable, they break. We know this. All evidence leads toward it. Small stopgap measures are put in place that allow the can to be kicked down the road another couple of blocks, but even that is not sustainable.

Be as prepared as possible for the turning point when it comes. Changes are going to happen, not because I say so but because history proves this. It's a proven fact that history repeats itself.

These are my observations. Those who disagree are either uninformed or simply being intellectually dishonest. It's politically expedient not to accept these premises, but there are mountains of tangible historic evidence to prove any of these realizations.

People say we're ruining the planet, but we don't have the ability to do that. When Mother Earth gets sick of us, She will sneeze, and we will go the way of the dinosaurs. We fancy ourselves way too highly, and it will ultimately destroy us. After all, humans aren't at the top of the food chain: viruses are.

IT IS HUMAN TO ERR; TO FORGIVE, DIVINE

I enjoy the freedom both to succeed and to fail. One of my favorite philosophical quotes, roughly translated, is, 'That which doesn't destroy you makes you stronger,' and I totally believe that, one hundred percent, because you learn from your mistakes. I've learned from my mistakes, and it's been a great motivator.

When you make a mistake, oftentimes there's some kind of pain that goes along with it, whether it's physical or financial or whatever, and then you know to dial in some of your choices a little bit better, hopefully. But when you have paternalistic institutions—governmental, mainly—that take the pain out of these things, it's easy to abdicate responsibility for your own life to someone else, then it's never your fault.

As a result, you don't learn from your mistakes, and you don't ultimately evolve and become a better person. You get in patterns, and you know there's never going to be a time when you make a choice and you're going to have food on the table or not.

Back when Germany was in two parts, the East Germans had a particular wing of the government called the Stasi. They encouraged their neighbors to spy on each other and report everything that they did. That came to be frowned upon by the West, but it's what we're doing now on Facebook. We're doing it willingly.

All the things that people fought to overcome, we're rebuilding the notion of that though social media. We're happily marching to the slaughter—we're not being corralled unwillingly into it. We're all jovial, we're singing drinking songs, all the merry way.

THE LONE STAR STATE

I now live in an amazing place, generally speaking. I've come to feel that Texas has an attitude. Over and above the particular artistic and creative thing that is very prevalent in the Austin area, there has historically been this attitude in the state of Texas that is really self-reliant and independent. This state was born of those very convictions, and it's a shared mentality.

I'm not saying everyone here is like that, but the majority of the folks who you meet here can identify with that. You can sense that by the patriotism toward the state that the residents feel. Anybody who comes and visits here and notices the number of state flags on people's houses or bumper stickers on their cars, will realize that those people are very pro-Texas. That's confined to this state. You won't see that in any other state in the country. In fact, some entire countries don't have this symbolism.

Texas was its own country at one time, and it's certainly big enough to be one—it's bigger than many countries—and there's an awareness of that. It's a prideful attitude, and you sense it in day-to-day life here. I've always felt that attitude inside, and it's nice that I'm not all alone in that. I'm living among a population where that's an underlying definition of what it is to be a Texan, as well as an American. It's not just a school, it's an attitude of rolling up your sleeves and getting it done, and there's a defiance as well. Texas was born of this attitude, and I'm doing my part to ensure it remains that way.

I can see parallels there with Morbid Angel—that strength and conviction. Strength through confidence. Strength through achievement. Achievement in the face of overwhelming odds. Forging a path that had not already been paved by someone else. All of these things are a big part of my character, and I'm very comfortable with that.

THE POWER OF ADVERSITY

Adversity is a good motivator, because it helps you to recognize what the pattern of success is, and how it is made up of comedy and tragedy. There's a play, an obstacle, and by determination and hard work and the strength of conviction you find a way to get through that obstacle—whether that means running right through it, tunneling under it, or going around it or over it, you find a way to overcome that obstacle and even make it a friend.

If it's something that has caused you to alter an approach to a problem in such a way where that type of obstacle will never be an obstacle again, then it has taught you a lesson. You can then use it as a tool in your toolbox of life to navigate through a situation that may be similar. I like that.

These are all character-building things, and there's a feeling of satisfaction that comes when you've earned or achieved something the hard way. Things are much more important to me when I've worked for them, and seen something come to fruition because I deliberately went after it, cared about it, and bent my will toward it. I took the steps and kept it in focus and worked it until it bore fruit. There's a satisfaction that comes from the earning of these successes that makes them that much sweeter.

WILL I EVER ENTER POLITICS?

No. Any musings that I may have had on the subject of entering politics have already been ruined by my past. I'd be starting off on a very imbalanced footing. Imagine me being a politician—a guy who sings about the destruction of religion with conviction. That would make me a nonstarter. Thankfully, I'm not interested in entering politics, but if I were, that alone would make it a bad idea.

AMERICA

I've asked myself the question of where I would live if I lived outside the USA. Where else would I go? And who am I as a person, and what types of adjustments would I need to make to define myself with the things that are important to me? What things would I have to give up, and what changes would I have to make, in order to live elsewhere?

I am an American and proud to be American. I'm not necessarily proud of some of the things that our government has chosen to do, and some of the things within our system that I think are fundamentally immoral or incorrect on the world stage. But from a standpoint of where I'm looking at my lifestyle, this is the best place for me, for those reasons. You grow up in a certain place and you come to respect certain things. Still, could I manage elsewhere? I could, yes, but would I choose to do so? I think not.

THE SUM OF HUMAN HAPPINESS

There's been a number of highs and lows over my life, rather than a period of time when I was the happiest I've been, or indeed the saddest. There is no comedy without tragedy; there is no right without wrong. It's two sides of the same coin, and this particular coin is my life.

When I look back at things in retrospect and think, *Well, if I would have done this, or if I would have made a different choice, there might have been a different outcome at certain points*, I tend to realize that all this was really part of a process; part of an ongoing story.

My today answer is that tomorrow I will be at my happiest. My tomorrow answer will hopefully be that the next day I will be at my happiest. I look at happiness and sadness the same way. They're both exponents of living life as a dynamic individual who makes choices like everyone else every day, but I have to welcome a volume level of one in order to appreciate a volume level of ten.

GOALS

What am I seeking? I don't think that there's any one thing that I'm looking for. I think everyone can relate to this answer. Ultimately, we all like peace and security and happiness, and a sense of accomplishment. Everyone has the same basic needs. We want to be at a point where we know that we're going to have food and shelter, and however we each define love and happiness in our own lives.

Everything plays off of that and is a continuance of these things, and my philanthropic side can exist because I've found good places where now I'm complete—and I feel good about sharing some of those ideas with others.

I remember when I was a kid, you couldn't tell me a thing. I knew everything. The older I get, the dumber I get, which is really not the truth, but the more I know, the more that I know what I don't know.

TRAVEL

Do I miss being in Morbid Angel? No, I don't miss the situation that I left at all. The songs that I wrote and recorded are very dear to my heart, but at the same time I don't do things that are halfhearted. Being a performer is a huge part of my life, and I still have the hunger to do it, but I'm not interested in doing things that look like what I've been doing for the past few years.

The notion of going on tour for three months on a conveyor belt—I don't have any interest in doing that. I will always be a performer, but I'll probably relax the schedule a little bit and build in some time so that I can actually enjoy each day on tour as much as I would enjoy a day in my life anywhere I am.

I'd like to be less rigorous when I travel, so that if there's a place I'd like to visit, there will be a few days built in where I can do that, rather than just blowing through and only seeing an airport and a hotel and a venue. That gets a little old. I sit in the transport between the hotel and the venue and say, 'That looks interesting. I wonder what this is about? Maybe there's an excellent restaurant that I could visit, or some nature activity that I could put time into.'

We definitely have a very dynamic planet, and I sometimes feel that I'm cheating myself out of the opportunity to experience things in a little more depth than just blowing through as part of a tour. I have to hurry up and get to the next place, and when I'm there I have to hurry up to get to the place after that, so we all get home, and then you get a check and it starts again.

I'm bored with that, but only with that side of it. Every day is a day of life, and there are ways that I'm looking at to make some of these things a little more complete.

I know it's achievable. It would give me the opportunities to spend some time embracing new things. When I say that I've traveled the world, which I have, there's a lot of places that I'd like to spend a little more time in. If the folks in a certain area have been responsive to my music over the years, then maybe I can be a little more responsive to the culture of the local area and get to know a little bit more about them. I've started doing it recently, within the past few years, when there's been a one-off show or something on the tail end of something. Then I can find a way to spend an extra few days or a week getting to see more of an area than usual on tour.

THE GREAT OUTDOORS

I love nature. Anything that has to do with nature and being outdoors, I love. I love whitewater rafting, hiking, hunting, fishing—anything that involves interacting with nature, because it's very relaxing, and it brings me the perspective that we're part of this process. We live on a beautiful planet, but you lose that perspective if you spend most of your days in a large city as just another consumer.

Not that I don't consume, but it's nice to recognize this, and spend time away from all that, and do things like camping and riding motorcycles through the countryside. I relieve stress that way. It gives me lots of time for productive internal dialogue. I'm inspired about it, and it makes its way into every bastion of my life, from songwriting to my worldview.

EQUIP YOURSELF TO SURVIVE

This has always been something that was important to me—ever since I was a kid in the Boy Scouts, where I learned a lot of survival skills and the code of honor and respect for nature.

I felt those things instinctually anyway, but this was an institution where kids have an opportunity to learn skills from tying knots to orienteering, or putting yourself in a situation where—if there were some sort of catastrophic thing, manmade or natural—you would have the skillset to do something beyond stampeding with your fellow citizens and looting a grocery store to try to take care of yourself.

Be able to grow your own food and be able to hunt. If there was no electricity and no telephone service and no automobiles or fuel, how are we prepared to fare under those circumstances? These are things that don't seem to be given that much importance in modern society, because people don't believe that it's necessary—because they think everything is too big to fail.

I don't know that the average city-dweller is really in touch with the type of thing I'm talking about. But it's important to me, and it's always been a big part of my life. It's part of my religious beliefs as well, that we are—like it or not, believe it or not—a part of nature, and when we lose sight of that it's not healthy.

Things could improve in this respect, because we humans have the ability to turn things around—but there's a problem ...

THE OBSTACLES TO PROGRESS

In our society, we have some of the greatest minds that have evolved from the Platos of the world. Each time someone takes over and improves upon the last guy's work, the next person after that takes over and improves exponentially on that achievement, and so we find ourselves doing some of these marvelous things that we're doing these days.

The flipside of that is that we're living in a world that somehow doesn't always embrace the best and brightest, and that spends an inordinate amount of resources placating the lowest common denominator. We have organized religions that are dubious at best, and the absolute opposite of the dreaming and the technology and the creativity that's going on in the advanced fields of mathematics and physics and medicine.

Those two elements, although they're both part of the human psyche, are clearly incompatible. This is going to have to be addressed because, as quickly as the sciences that we've just discussed are rapidly evolving in one direction, pop culture and religious extremism are dragging a large portion of the population downward.

A high percentage of people are not in the bell curve range of the folks who are leading the charge in the evolution that's taking us to new heights. That worries me.

CHOICES

You can choose your own logical path through all this. In life, you have an idea of what you'd like to do, but how do you get there? Some of my realizations have come from hard work, or mistakes, or meditation, or studying history, and some of these will be inspirational to others on their paths.

It's all a choice. I hear people complaining about what they do, and I always think, *Figure out what you want to do and do it. Take the necessary steps*. Everybody deserves to be happy, but you have to make it happen yourself. Ask yourself who you are. What fits you best? Don't look at employment solely as something that you have to do to pay the bills. Don't become a slave to something. Keep your eye on happiness; there's no reason to live a miserable life when we're only here for a very short period of time. It's up to us to make that time as enjoyable as possible for ourselves, and hopefully extend that to others.

DON'T BE CYNICAL

I believe in keeping an open mind. If I listen to music and I don't understand it, I want to make sure that I don't dismiss it. I'm in my fifties now, and it would be easy for me to be dismissive of that which I don't understand. Knowing this, and being well aware that this is the kind of thing that happens with age or unfamiliarity, I make a point of listening to music and trying to find out why it's popular.

I ask myself if I can feel those things, or share them. At the very least, I will give it a chance. My decision may be that I don't like it, but I don't want to just write it off without giving it the same chance that I would have expected from folks listening to the music I make.

My mind is more open the older I get, because I've recognized that being closed leads to stagnation. I liken it to traveling. Being in a different country leads you to different languages and cultures, although music can transcend both of those in a lot of ways. That's part of my worldview now. I don't have the provincial view that so many people do, because it's not helpful.

You shouldn't dislike that which you don't know. You should be well informed, or inform yourself, as much as possible, and that way you can make more accurate distinctions within your own life about things that work and things that don't. I freely admit that there are things that don't work for me that would be the complete opposite for someone who has different tastes and viewpoints.

But none of this comes unless you consider it. You have to make a decision to do so.

CARPE DIEM

I don't want to be a passive participant in life. I want to be an active participant, even though it requires work on my part in order to do so. I feel much more enriched because I've taken this attitude; I feel that I've been able to share that enrichment and extend it to others by encouraging them not to be as I am, or to do the things I've done, but to find their own path.

I've made my share of mistakes, and I'm certainly no angel, but I'm morbid when it comes to this. By 'morbid' I mean 'death to small-mindedness' and 'death to mediocrity.' It's the antithesis to shuffling along and being ushered into settling for mediocrity.

Don't settle for that. Settle for nothing.

WHAT HAVE I LEARNED FROM MY LIFE SO FAR?

If I died tomorrow, I would die fulfilled. I feel that I've seen more, done more, and experienced more than ninety-nine percent of humanity, for which I'm truly thankful.

I also believe that, in a very simple way, immortality is certain. Bach, Wagner, Elvis—these people are all still alive, because they left an indelible mark in history that cannot be forgotten. This, along with their genetic lineage, frames the components of immortality. These are tangible things that cannot be denied, even though people add to them with their belief system.

I take the time to understand the basis of beliefs. I make quality observations, and reach quality conclusions, based on my own fundaments. I will always be rebellious at heart, but the things that once hampered me are no longer of any consequence. My approach may have started with simple rebellion, but I have found the answers to many of the questions that caused me to rebel in the first place.

You can find those answers too.

DISCOGRAPHY

MORBID ANGEL

1988............................'Thy Kingdom Come'
1989....................................*Altars Of Madness*
1991.................................. *Blessed Are The Sick*
1991.....................*Abominations Of Desolation*
1993... *Covenant*
1993... 'Rapture'
1994................................ 'God Of Emptiness'
1994......................................*Laibach Re-Mixes*
1995...*Domination*
1995...........................'Where The Slime Live'
1996...................................*Entangled In Chaos*
2011.............................*Illud Divinum Insanus*
2011... 'Nevermore'
2011....... *Illud Divinum Insanus—The Remixes*
2015..*Juvenilia*

GENITORTURERS

1998...*Sin City*
2000... *Machine Love*
2002...................................... *Flesh Is The Law*
2009................................*Blackheart Revolution*

TERRORIZER

1989... *World Downfall*
2012...................................*Hordes Of Zombies*

HEADCAT

2017.................... 'Born To Lose, Live To Win'

SOLO

2017....................... 'Drinkin' With The Devil'

VLTIMAS

2019.................. *Something Wicked Marches In*

SELECTED GUEST APPEARANCES

1998...............Acheron, *Those Who Have Risen*
2004............ Karl Sanders, *Saurian Meditation*
2008.......................................Soulfly, *Conquer*
2010............Team Cybergeist, *How To Destroy Something Beautiful*
2013.................................Chaostar, *Anomima*
2015.....................Melted Space, *The Great Lie*
2015.......................... Nuclear Chaos, *Suffocate*

INDEX

Except where indicated, all songs and albums listed here are by Morbid Angel.

Abbott, Darrell (*aka* Dimebag), 131, 176, 177, 178–9
Abbott, Vinnie Paul, 179
Abominations Of Desolation, 47, 48, 82, 83
Accept, 233
Aerosmith, 23
Aliens (movie), 66
Alighieri, Dante, 60
Altars Of Madness, 32, 33, 35, 56, 57, 59, 60, 66, 67, 76, 79, 82, 83, 94, 96, 200
'American Pie' (Don McLean song), 17
Angel, 55
Angel Witch, 55
Anselmo, Phil, 176, 213
Apocalypse Now (movie), 208
Apone, Sgt., 66
Arellano, Jaime Gomez, 217, 218
Atheist, 97
Atreyu, 187
Azagthoth, Trey, 47, 48, 49, 50, 54, 56, 62, 66, 76, 80, 81, 82, 87, 94, 96, 101, 103, 105, 117, 118, 171, 190, 194–5, 196, 197, 198, 199, 201, 202, 203, 223

Bach, Johann Sebastian, 267
Badu, Erykah, 25
Baltes, Peter, 233
Bathory, 44–5
Batio, Michael Angelo, 131
Beavan, Sean, 198
Beavis & Butt-Head (TV show), 95, 96, 111
Berberian, Michael, 219
Black Flag, 25
Black Sabbath, 17, 24, 27, 101, 241
'Black Sabbath' (Black Sabbath song), 238
Blessed Are The Sick, 63, 76, 79, 81, 82, 83, 84, 85, 86, 88, 94, 96, 110, 111, 158, 199, 200
'Blessed Are The Sick/Leading The Rats,' 82, 110–11
'Blood Fire War Hate' (Soulfly song), 186
Blood Of Kingu (ritual), 66–7
Blue Öyster Cult, 23
Blues Brothers, The (movie), 25
Blythe, Randy, 213
Bolt Thrower, 72, 97
Book Of Lies, The (book), 147
'Brainstorm,' 85-86
Branson, Sir Richard, 182
Brecht, Eric, 49
Browning, Mike, 47
Brunelle, Richard, 47, 48, 49, 51, 81, 93, 94, 97
Buffalo Springfield, 24
Burns, Scott, 76
Burton, Cliff, 103
Butcher (dog), 34, 35, 66, 68, 69
Butler, Geezer, 233

'Caesar's Palace,' 137–38, 205–6
Caligula (movie), 206, 241
Carcass, 72, 73, 94, 97, 187
Cavalera, Max, 180, 185–6
Celtic Frost, 45
'Chapel Of Ghouls,' 54
Church Of Satan, 143, 145
Clinton, Bill, 67
Cogumelo (record label), 180
Columbia (record label), 94
Conquer (Soulfly album), 185, 186
Cooper, Alice, 23, 27, 125, 127, 128, 233
Copeland, Miles, 125
Copeland, Stewart, 125
Copenhell (festival), 219
Covenant, 93, 94, 95, 96, 99, 105, 114, 135–6, 198, 199, 200, 223
Crowley, Aleister, 115, 146
Cryptopsy, 216
Cult, The, 97

'Damnation,' 60–2
Danzig, Glenn, 101
Dark Angel, 55
'Dawn Of The Angry,' 167–9
'Day Of Suffering,' 88–9
'Dead Shall Rise' (Terrorizer song), 76
Dean Guitars, 98, 130–1, 176, 182, 235
Death Angel, 55
Death (*aka* Mantas), 46
Death Race 2000 (movie), 24
Deep Purple, 23, 25
Deicide, 97
Delville, Jean, 63, 79
De Sade, Marquis Donatien, 125, 146, 206–7
Destruction, 45
Devil Worship: Exposing Satan's Underground (TV documentary), 69
'Diabolus Est Sanguis' (Vltimas song), 250–1
Dickinson, Bruce, 187
Disney, 17
Disturbed, 238
'Dominate,' 137–8
Domination, 94, 97, 101, 103, 106, 137, 138, 163, 164, 167, 200, 204, 205, 207, 209, 210, 223
Douglas, Carl, 24

DRI, 49
'Drinkin' With The Devil' (David Vincent song), 213–4, 247–9
Dunaway, Dennis, 233

Earache (record label), 37, 56, 72, 74, 78, 79, 83, 94, 95, 203
Easy Rider (movie), 24
Emerson, Keith, 46
Entangled In Chaos, 108–9
Entombed, 78, 97, 150
Entwistle, John, 234
Eriksen, Rune, 216, 217, 238, 239
'Evil Spells,' 54
'Existo Vulgoré,' 220–1
'Eyes To See, Ears To Hear,' 163–4

'Fall From Grace,' 63–4, 82, 200
Fight, 186
Ford, Gunter, 78, 79, 95, 96, 97, 100, 101, 105, 117, 118, 124, 171, 173, 189
Forsberg, Tomas (*aka* Quorthon), 45
Freeman, Gene (*aka* Machine), 249
Frontier Booking (agency), 125

Garcia, Oscar, 76
Genitorturers, 91, 108, 115, 124, 125, 126, 176
Ghost, 218
Giant (label), 95, 100, 101, 102
'Girls, Girls, Girls' (Mötley Crüe song), 43
Godflesh, 91
'God Of Emptiness,' 95, 96, 111, 135, 199, 201
Golgotha (movie), 237
Gonzalez, Juan (*aka* Punchy) 190-191, 196, 224
Gore, Al, 67
Gore, Tipper, 67
Goreque Records (label), 45
Grand Funk Railroad, 23, 27, 233, 241
Graspop (festival), 108
Grave, 78
Grindcrusher (tour), 33, 72, 73

Hair Metal Zombie Massacre (movie), 213
Halford, Rob, 186–7
Hammer Films (horror movies), 23
Harris, Lauren, 187
Harris, Mick, 55, 72, 74
Harris, Steve, 50, 233
Hartsell, Wayne, 48, 49, 50, 51
Harvey, Danny, 214, 248, 249
Hate Eternal, 181
'Hatework,' 209–10
Headbangers Ball (TV show), 102
Headcat, 214, 215, 237
Heavy Metal (compilation album), 23
Hell Awaits (Slayer album), 47
Hellfest (festival), 152, 219
Hellhammer, 45
Hendrix, Jimi, 17
Heretic, 171
Heston, Charlton, 218, 219
Hetfield, James, 84
Hurricane Katrina, 15

I Am Morbid, 215
'I Am Morbid,' 224–6
Illud Divinum Insanus, 194, 195, 198, 199, 200, 201, 220, 221, 224, 244
Illud Divinum Insanus—The Remixes, 202
'I Love The Dead' (Alice Cooper song), 23
'Immortal Rites,' 32, 54, 56, 200
Inferno (poem), 60
'Inquisition (Burn With Me),' 138, 207–9
I.N.R.I. (Sarcofago album), 180
Iron Cross, 25
Iron Maiden, 24, 40, 50, 187, 233
IRS (label), 125

Jett, Joan, 97
Jobs, Steve, 182
Judas Priest, 24, 97, 186, 187
Judge, Mike, 111
Juvenilia, 203

Kennedy, Bill, 101
Kilgore, Lieutenant Colonel Bill, 208
Kilmister, Ian (*aka* Lemmy), 214
King, B.B., 25
Kingston Trio, The, 27
KISS, 23, 25, 126, 233
Kollias, George, 193, 194
Korn, 96
'Kung Fu Fighting' (Carl Douglas song), 24

Laibach, 100, 195
Laibach Re-Mixes, 100
Lamb Of God, 213, 249
Lamounier, Wagner, 180
'Last Ones Alive Win Nothing' (Vltimas song), 218
LaVey, Anton, 143, 145
Leary, Timothy, 92
Led Zeppelin, 23, 25
Lee, Christopher, 23
Lemmy, *see* Kilmister, Ian
Les Trésors De Satan (painting), 80
Lewis, Annie Marie, 248, 249
Liebert, Ottmar, 181
Lombardo, Dave, 49
Loomis, Roland (*aka* Fakir Musafar), 114–15
'Lord Of All Fevers And Plagues,' 54, 62
Lords Of The New Church, 125
Lovecraft, H.P., 80, 87–8, 146
Lusitania (ship), 134

Machine Love (Genitorturers album), 125
Mad Max (movies), 156
Magickal Childe (bookstore), 70
MaidenFest (festival), 187
Mana Studios, 181
Mantas, *see* Death
'Marching On' (Vltimas song), 217
Mayhem, 216
'Maze Of Torment,' 54, 59–60, 200
McCartney, Sir Paul, 231–2
McDonald's, 13, 14, 23, 169
McLean, Don, 17
Megadeth, 249
Mercyful Fate, 44
Metallica, 43, 84, 96
Metal Maniacs (magazine), 49
Metoyer, Bill, 47
Minor Threat, 25
Misfits, The, 25
Modern Primitives (magazine), 115
Monk (TV show), 118
Monsanto, 37
Monty Python (comedy group), 209
Morbid Angel, 29, 33, 45, 47, 48, 54, 55, 56, 57, 66, 70, 72, 74, 76, 80, 82, 91, 94, 96, 97, 98, 99, 104, 107, 108, 117, 124, 127, 131, 142, 144, 150, 171, 172, 173, 178, 180, 190, 192, 194, 195, 199, 201, 202, 203, 212, 213, 215, 223, 228, 235, 258, 261
Morris, Tom, 56
Morrisound Studio, 56, 96, 101
Mötley Crüe, 43
MTV, 102
Mounier, Flo, 216, 217
Myhren, Thor (*aka* Destructhor), 190, 191, 196, 197
Myrkskog, 190
Mystic Fest (festival), 219

Napalm Death, 56, 72, 74, 75, 76, 91, 94, 97
Neat Records (label), 55
Necronomicon (book), 87–8
'Nevermore,' 191, 199
Nietzsche, Friedrich, 147
Nile, 43, 193
Nine Inch Nails, 124
Nitro, 131
Norman, Tony, 171–2, 173–4, 181
'Nothing But Fear,' 164–6
Nugent, Ted, 23
Nu-metal, 106
NWA, 25

Obama, Barack, 142
Obituary, 97
Ohio Players, The, 25
Omega Man, The (movie), 218
'Omni Potens,' 195
Ortega, John, 47
Osbourne, Ozzy, 201
Overlourd, 40, 41, 43
Ozzfest, 214, 215

'Pain Divine,' 111, 114
Pantera, 176
Paradise Lost, 218
'Paranoid' (Black Sabbath song), 24, 201
Parents' Music Resource Center, the (PMRC), 67
Pearson, Digby, 37, 56, 72, 76, 79, 94, 95, 100
Pink Floyd, 196
Pinochet, Augusto, 175
Pintado, Jesse, 51, 52, 76
Plato, 264
Police, The, 125
Possessed, 45
Powell, Cozy, 197
Presley, Elvis, 267
Price, Vincent, 23
'Profundis—Mea Culpa,' 244–6

Quorthon, *see* Forsberg, Tomas
'Radikult,' 199
'Rapture,' 95, 111, 200
Rammstein, 100
Rasmussen, Flemming, 96
Realm Of The Damned (movie), 237
'Rebel Lands,' 86–7
Relativity Records, 79
Reznor, Trent, 101, 124
Ride The Lightning (Metallica album), 43
Ripping Corpse, 96
Rivera, Geraldo, 69, 70
Rizzo, Marc, 181
Robbins, Tony, 147
Rock, Bob, 84
Rubinson, Elliott, 98, 182, 235
Rutan, Erik, 94, 96, 101, 174, 181, 188, 194, 196, 210

Sadus, 97
Sanders, Karl, 43, 131, 194
Sandoval, Pete, 51, 52, 53, 54, 62, 66, 67, 76, 81, 92, 106, 171, 190, 191, 192, 193, 194
Sarcofago, 180
Sarzo, Rudy, 55
Satanic Bible, The (book), 143
Savatage, 56
Schacher, Mel, 233
Schuldiner, Chuck, 46, 47, 49, 236
Scorpions, 40
Scream Forth Blasphemies, 47
Seagrave, Dan, 57
Season Of Mist (label), 217, 219
Sepultura, 180
Sesame Street (TV show), 17
Simmons, Gene, 126–7, 233
Sin City (Genitorturers album), 125
Slayer, 47, 49
Something Wicked Marches In (Vltimas album), 216, 250
'Something Wicked Marches In' (Vltimas song), 217
Soulfly, 180, 181, 185

'Sound Of Silence, The' (Simon & Garfunkel song), 238
Spock, Mr., 151
Star Licks (instructional video), 131
Star Trek (TV show), 9, 151
Star Wars (movie), 24
Steppenwolf, 23
Sunn O))), 218
'Suffocation,' 33–4, 54
Sweden Rock (festival), 97–8
Sweet Silence (studio), 96
'Sworn To The Black,' 111

Terrorizer, 51, 52, 76, 193
Terrorizer (magazine), 82
Texas Chainsaw Massacre, The (movie), 24
'This Means War,' 204–5
'Thy Kingdom Come,' 50, 111–13
Tons Of Rock (festival), 219
'Too Extreme!,' 199, 200, 221–3
Tucker, Steve, 171
Turner, Nick, 125

Ultimas, *see* Vltimas
Unleashed, 78, 97

Vanishing Point (movie), 24
Vargas, Josh, 213, 214
Venom, 44
Vietnam War, 25
Vincent, David: birth, 12; parents' background and employment, 12; brothers, 12, 19–20; on hunting, 13, 14; on nature, 13, 14, 262–3; on nutrition, 14, 73–4; bitten by rattlesnake, 15–17; musical influences, 18, 23, 25; grade school, 18–19; misbehavior at school, 20–2; on drugs, 22, 91, 92, 93; taste in films, 24; music studies, 26, 27–8; on acting, 26–7; disagreement and reconciliation with father, 29–31, 39; leaving school and home, 29–31; early bands, 40, 42, 45; college, 41–2; on California, 44; starting Goreque Records, 45; joining Morbid Angel in 1986, 48; move to Florida, 50; on travel, 57–8, 152–4, 261–2; encounters with the police, 68–9, 70, 71–2, 160, 182–5; on relationships, 75; on touring, 77, 78; injuries and illnesses, 77–8, 188; on religion, 89, 142–6, 147–50, 226, 253–4; personal development, 98, 99, 103–6, 117–18, 120–4, 131, 173, 179–80, 216; leaving Morbid Angel in 1996, 108; marriage to Gen, 119–20; Evil D. nickname, 125; wrestling promotions, 128–30; on government, 142, 149; on racism, 150–1; on vehicles, 154–62; rejoining Morbid Angel in 2004, 172; leaving Morbid Angel in 2015, 202; playing country music, 212–13; on songwriting, 228, 231–2, 238–41; musical equipment, 233–5; on Texas, 257–8
Vincent, Gen, 39, 91, 106, 114, 115, 118, 119, 120, 124, 125, 126, 127, 131, 171
'Visions From The Dark Side,' 35–7, 54
Vltimas, 15, 216, 217, 219, 231, 238, 239, 251
Voivod, 45, 196

Wacken Festival, 214, 219
Wagner, Richard, 218, 267
Wakeman, Rick, 46
Warfare Noise (compilation album), 180
Warner Music Group (label), 95, 138
Warwick, Vanessa, 108
Welcome To My Nightmare (Alice Cooper album), 23
'Where The Slime Live,' 101, 138, 139–40
Woodstock (1969 festival), 25, 91
World Downfall (Terrorizer album), 76
World Trade Center attacks, 132–4

Yes, 23, 241
Yeung, Tim, 194, 195, 196, 197, 198, 216

Zelinsky, Dean, 176–7
Zyklon, 190

PICTURE CREDITS

All photographs featured in this book are from the author's collection, except: *Morbid bus, 1988 rehearsal*, Edward Morgan; *Michigan (x3)*, *Poughkeepsie*, *Milwaukee*, Frank White Photography; *With Full Force*, *Graspop*, *Wacken*, Martin Wickler; *Irving Plaza*, *Anaheim*, Rodrigo Fredes (Photo Terco); *Slim's*, Steven Chew; *Drinkin'*, Suzanne Penley; *White Horse Saloon*, Jim Wilkinson; *Whisky*, Dana Osgood; *Alcatraz*, Jesus Martinez; *Vltimas*, Tina Korhonen; *Fonda Theater*, Chris Loomis; *Islington Academy*, Ester Segarra/Metal Hammer.